Studies of the Yaqui Indians of Sonora, Mexico

The History, Culture and Anthropology of the Yaqui Native Americans

By William Curry Holden

Professor of History and Anthropology and Director of
Archaeological Research, Texas Technological College

PANTIANOS
CLASSICS

Published by Pantianos Classics

ISBN-13: 978-1-78987-486-0

First published in 1936

Contents

Acknowledgements

The following studies of the Yaqui Indians are by no means exhaustive, and the members of the expedition are fully aware that more remains to be said on the various subjects treated by them than they have included in these reports. The various papers, with the exception of Dr. Seltzer's, have been written with the layman in view rather than the professional anthropologist.

We wish to express our appreciation to the civil and military officials of the Republic of Mexico for their kindness and cooperation in making the expedition possible: to Mr. Ramón Beteta, Director General of Statistics, for his friendly interest; to Mr. José Reygadas Vértiz, Head of the Departments of Monuments, for giving us permission to make ethnological studies among the Yaquis; to Manuel Mascarenas, Jr., Chief of Customs at Nogales, Sonora, for extending to us the "courtesy of the port", both on entering and leaving Mexico; to General Jesus Gutiérrez Cázares, Lt. Colonel Francisco Salcedo, and Lt. Colonel Natividad Jácome, Mexican officers in the Yaqui region of Sonora, for military assistance and courtesies; to José Miranda, Yaqui governor of Torin, and the other Yaqui chiefs at Vicam and Torin for their friendly cooperation; and to Ramón Torry, our Yaqui interpreter, for his faithful service and personal loyalty to the members of the staff.

For financial support and contribution of supplies we are indebted to the Rotary Club of Lubbock, the Kiwanis Club of Lubbock, the West Texas Chamber of Commerce, the *Lubbock Avalanche,* the *Amarillo Globe News,* Davis and Humphrey Wholesale Grocery Company of Lubbock, Swift and Company of Lubbock, Western Windmill Company of Lubbock, J. A. Folger and Company of Kansas City and San Francisco, Texas Power and Light Company, Mr. John W. Carpenter of Dallas, Mr. Spencer Wells of Lubbock, and to many other organizations and individuals.

We wish to thank Mrs. R. A. Studhalter, Mrs. W. C. Holden, Professor Gus L. Ford, and Professor C. D. Eaves for taking over the routine college work of two members of the staff while those individuals were on the expedition. We are indebted to Miss Elizabeth Howard West for having read the several manuscripts.

W. C. Holden

Director of the Yaqui Expedition

Introduction

William Curry Holden, Director

Our active interest in the Yaqui Indians began in the spring of 1933. Through Miss Yone Stone of Lubbock we met Mr. Ivan Williams, an immigration officer from Marfa, Texas. Mr. Williams for several years had been closely associated with a group of Yaqui refugees at Tucson, Arizona. During a period of Yaqui hostilities in 1926 this group had been driven across the border by a superior Mexican force. Mr. Williams befriended the refugees and in time won their confidence. They elected him an honorary chief and gave him a chief's staff and feather bonnet.

By talking with the old men, Williams learned that Yaquis had long kept a "history" of their tribe handed down by word of mouth. He asked "General" Guadalupe Flores, chief of the refugees, to send word down to the chiefs of the Yaqui villages on the Rio Yaqui in Sonora requesting them to have some of their history written down and sent to Tucson. There is constant communication between the Arizona Yaquis and the Yaquis of Sonora. Runners slip back and forth over secret trails between the Bacatete Mountains and the border. The Sonora chiefs decided to supply the "history." They directed one of their tribe who could operate a typewriter to write the tribal traditions as dictated by the old men. The scribe wrote a few episodes and attempted to send them to Arizona through the Mexican mails. The Mexicans intercepted the letters, and the Yaquis tried another plan. They typed a chapter on cloth, sewed it in the lining of a shirt, put the shirt on a runner who carried it over the secret trails to Tucson. Williams said that every few weeks a runner would arrive at Tucson with a "shirt full of history". It was written in Yaqui. "General" Flores would translate it into Spanish, and Williams in turn would translate it into English. In all there were about 8,000 words of it.

Five months later Mr. Williams was kind enough to let us see the account. It was mostly a sketchy account of the tribal wars with the Mexicans since 1740. It occurred to us that if we could get to the old men on the Rio Yaqui we could possibly draw from them additional information.

Williams had visited the eight villages on the Rio Yaqui in 1929, and had become a close friend of Jesus Munguia, at that time chief of all the villages. Munguia had since urged Williams to visit the Yaquis again and bring his friends if he wished. An opportunity to enter the Yaqui country as "Williams' friends" caused us to start planning an expedition.

The matter of financing an expedition in 1933 was a serious one. The depression was at its worst, many banks were closed, and funds of foundations for scientific work had been greatly decreased through the stock market collapse. Finally, we worked out a plan to finance the expedition locally. President Bradford Knapp and the Board of Directors of Texas Technological Col-

v

lege enthusiastically approved of the project. *The Avalanche Journal* undertook to sponsor the campaign. Service clubs, business firms, and the West Texas Chamber of Commerce contributed more readily than we anticipated.

The director of the expedition, accompanied by his wife, went to Mexico City during the Christmas holidays, 1933, and secured not only permission, but the cooperation of the Mexican government. Mexican officials listened to our story and became quite interested in our proposed expedition. They frankly admitted that the Yaquis had been terribly abused by the Spanish government and by the Mexican government until a few years ago. Porfirio Diaz had tried to exterminate them. At the present the government seems to want to do the right thing by the Yaquis.

During January and February of 1934 we organized our expedition. We wished to make historical, physical anthropological, archaeological, ethnological, ethnobotanical, herpetological, ornithological, and medical investigations. To this end Harvard University attached to our staff a physical anthropologist, Dr. Carl Coleman Seltzer, student of Dr. E. A. Hooton. Dr. Richard A. Studhalter, head of the Department of Biology, Texas Technological College, accepted our invitation to go as ethnobotanist. Dr. Charles J. Wagner, chief of staff of the West Texas Hospital, was selected to care for the health of the party and investigate Yaqui diseases. To William G. McMillan of Lubbock was entrusted the study of wild life. Charles A. Guy, editor and publisher of the *Avalanche Journal,* was to assist in recording data. Bennie McWilliams, a Technological College student, was added as cook and assistant archaeologist. At the last moment the expedition decided to take along Ross Edwards and Frank Maddox of Lubbock as outdoor men and camp assistants. We were desirous to add a geologist, but we had been repeatedly told by persons who knew that the Yaquis are jealously guarding their minerals and that one man examining rocks and geological structures would jeopardize the entire expedition.

Our party left Lubbock March 1, travelling in two cars and a heavily loaded truck. That night we camped at Van Horn where we had a long interview with Mr. Williams. We had hoped to take him with us, but he was unable to get a leave at the time. He had already written "General" Flores that we were coming by way of Tucson and had asked him to give us a letter to Jesus Munguia.

When we arrived at Tucson, Flores was expecting us. We camped from Saturday until Monday in the center of Pascua village where we got considerable information from Flores and others concerning conditions in the Yaqui country. Flores spent the most of Sunday preparing a letter for us to take to Munguia.

At Nogales the Mexican immigration and customs officials gave us every consideration. Our letters from the government at Mexico City had the desired effect. The chief of the customs service extended us "the courtesy of the port", kept the custom house open three quarters of an hour overtime in order that we might not lose an hour's driving, did not inspect a thing we had, and gave us a letter to keep any one else from inspecting us along the road.

Our route took us to Hermosillo, Guaymas, and then east into the Yaqui country. We stayed a week at Vicam and three weeks at Torin from which place we made short visits to Potam and Consica.

The Rio Yaqui rises in southern Arizona, flows south approximately 300 miles and then turns west some 90 miles into the Gulf of California. The eight historic Yaqui villages were scattered at more or less equal intervals along the lower 90 mile stretch of the river which extended from east to west. [1] The country on either side of the river from ten to twelve miles is low and flat, and of a sedimentary, sandy loam, covered with a dense growth of mesquite trees and cacti. A few isolated, rugged hills with elevations from 100 to 200 feet are scattered between the river and the Bacatete Mountains to the north. Occasionally there will be hundreds of acres of *cholla* so thick neither man nor horse can penetrate the thickets. Organ pipe cacti and *sahuaras* of great size are plentiful. All the vegetation is of a semi-desert nature. There is little rain in the region from October until June, and none too much from June to October.

Dr. Studhalter made observations of the temperature of the region. He reports: "The temperature is hot in summer, and frosts are rare in winter. At Vicam and Torin, from March 8 to April 3, 1934, temperature records were taken each day, when possible, at about 8 A.M., at noon and again at 6 P.M. The morning temperatures ranged from 50° to 68° F., with a mean of 58°. At noon, the range was found to be from 75° to 93° F., with a mean of 82°. The mean late afternoon record was 77° F., with a range from 69° to 87°. During the same period, the morning relative humidity ranged from 25 to 71 p.c. with a mean of 45 p.c. At noon the range was from 22 to 51 p. c., with a mean of 35 p.c.; and in the late afternoon, from 22 to 50 p.c., with a mean of 36 p.c. . Little variation was found in barometric pressure during the day, or from day to day."

Some fifteen miles north of the Rio Yaqui are the Bacatete Mountains, which extend about twenty-five miles east and west and about sixty north and south. Passes into the mountains are few, difficult and easily guarded from above. Ten men in the mountains can defend the passes against hundreds below by rolling rocks down on them. The Yaquis have from time immemorial held these mountains and are still holding them today. They will never be completely conquered so long as they continue to occupy them.

Dr. Alex Hrdlička visited four of the Yaqui villages in 1902. [2] He reported approximately 20,000 Yaquis living in the eight villages at the time. Dr. E. L. Hewitt was in the vicinity in 1906, but as yet has not published his observations. Today there are approximately 2600 Yaquis living in five villages. Extending from east to west, are Consica, Torin, Vicam (Old Vicam), and Potam. A remnant of the Cocorit Indians are located at the railroad town of Vicam.

The Yaquis of Agua Berde are defiant of all Mexican authority. They control the mountains and live mostly by stealing and by raiding outlying Mexican settlements. The Yaquis in the four river villages present a unique political situation. Six years ago the Mexican government changed its policy toward them. The government made a treaty with the Yaquis whereby each man would become technically a member of the Mexican army and receive forty-two pesos a month. Officers were to be paid on the same scale as Mexican officers. In this way the men of the river villages became a part of the army. However, they do not drill and do not take orders from the regular Mexican officers. In each village there are two garrisons, one Mexican, one Yaqui. They are paid by the same government, but spend their days watching each other. At night they mount guard against each other. There is a sort of invisible boundary line between them. The relations between the Yaqui chiefs and the Mexican officers are diplomatic.

We were not able to make contact with Jesus Munguia. He refused to comply with the last treaty between the Yaquis and the Mexican government. For the past five years he has been the chief of the Mountain Yaquis. As we were under the constant surveillance of the Mexican army we had no opportunity to arrange a meeting with Munguia. The mountain Yaquis are regarded by the Mexican government as outlaws and are shot on sight. The army guards the lower ends of the passes in an effort to prevent communication between the mountain Yaquis and those in the river villages. We ascertained, however, that the two groups have an understanding between them, and that the river Yaquis help to support the mountain people.

Our ethnological work during our first expedition was handicapped by the lack of adequate interpreters. At Tucson we had been told by Flores that we could find Yaquis at the villages who spoke English. Several days of searching in the four villages revealed one such man, Ramón Torry, and his knowledge of English was scant. He had gone to school in Tucson and had reached the third grade. Because of lack of an adequate interpreter we decided to confine the ethnological work to material culture and such phases of social culture as we might get by observation.

In September, 1934, three members of the first expedition, accompanied by Dr. Charles B. Qualia, head of the Foreign Language Department of Texas Technological College, as interpreter, made a second expedition to the Yaqui country. Dr. Studhalter went along to observe the fall agricultural crops and methods of harvesting. Dr. Wagner wished to continue his medical studies. With a competent interpreter we were desirous of investigating more thoroughly the social ethnology of the Yaquis. Dr. Qualia proved to be an excellent interpreter. He had been reared on the Mexican border and was familiar with the folk ways of Mexico. Furthermore his skill in framing questions and his ability to draw information from the Yaquis without the use of "lead questions" were comparable to those of a professional ethnologist. All our time during the second expedition was spent at Torin. We already had the confidence of the people at that village and we thought it best to concentrate our efforts there.

Perhaps our greatest single achievement was the contacts we made at Torin. Because of a series of fortunate incidents we made as much headway getting the confidence and cooperation of the people as we might have made in many months or years. We hope to make other expeditions in the future. If we do, we feel that we shall receive a genuine welcome, especially at Torin.

The expedition secured 144 museum specimens, 71 for Peabody Museum at Harvard and 73 for the Plains Museum Society at Texas Technological College. The two collections are for the most part duplicates and represent fairly well the articles used by the modern Yaqui. In addition a small collection of botanical specimens was made.

Dr. Wagner and Dr. Studhalter took approximately 600 pictures. Dr. Seltzer, in addition to photographing the 100 individuals whose measurements he took, made over 100 pictures dealing with Yaqui life. Dr. Wagner took 1200 feet of movie film. Mr. McMillan made numerous sketches, some of which are given in Plates 8, 9, 10.

[1] The historic villages from west to east were Belem (Mule Deer) Huiris, Rajum, Potam (Pocket Gopher), Vicam (Arrowhead), Torin (Big Mouse), Bacum (Water Hole), and Cocorit (Chili Pepper).
[2] Hrdlička, Ales, "Notes on the Indians of Sonora". *American Anthropologist,* 6:51—89, 1904.
    Hrdlička, Ales, "Physiological and Medical Observations among the Indians of Southwestern United States." *Bureau of American Ethnology Bulletin 34,* 1908.

Chapter One - Organizations

William Curry Holden

Political

The political system of the Yaquis is simple, definite, and effective. Each village has a governor elected for one year. About December 10 of each year the people, both men and women, of each village, gather for the election. The attendance at the election is compulsory. The army chief sends out details to bring in all truants. The proceedings are extremely informal. By agreement the people try to arrive at a selection. It sometimes requires a week of consultation to do this. When a decision has been reached, a committee waits on the one selected and informs him that he has been chosen. It seems to be a universal custom for no one to seek an office. When one is elected he usually pleads with the committee to choose another. The committee reasons with him and tells him that it is his duty to take the office. There is no getting out of it. We were told of instances where the one chosen was whipped until he accepted the place.

The functions of the governor are many and varied, — executive, diplomatic, legislative, judicial, social, and religious. [1] As an executive, he takes the initiative in the enforcement of tribal custom, which has the force of law. In his diplomatic capacity he speaks for the village in all negotiations with the other villages. Although the Mexican government does not technically recognize Yaqui autonomy to any degree, as a practical matter of administration it does recognize Yaqui autonomy in a *quasi* sense, and interferes with Yaqui affairs as little as possible. When the commandant of a Mexican garrison in a Yaqui village wishes something of the Yaquis, he sends for the governor and treats with him instead of issuing a military order as is usual in dealing with people under military rule. When measures are to be deliberated upon and policies formed the governor calls the men of the village together, and acts as a presiding officer when the matter is being discussed. He acts as a judge in both civil and criminal matters. In social affairs, the people of the village wait for the governor to take the lead. In all religious services the governor, assistant governors, ex-governors, and ex-assistant governors constitute an order or group with special functions.

There are four assistant governors elected in the same way and at the same time as the governor. They are designated as second governor, third governor, fourth governor, and fifth governor. Their functions are largely advisory. They constitute a sort of cabinet without individual portfolios so far as executive, diplomatic, legislative, social, and religious affairs are concerned. When judicial matters are at hand they, in conjunction with the governor, constitute a court. The duties of the fifth governor differ somewhat from those of the other three assistant governors. He is a sort of bailiff, sergeant at arms, or constable for the governor. As a badge of office he carries a rawhide whip tied around his waist. The whip is not altogether an insignia but also an implement of punishment. On occasion he lays it lustily upon the bare backs of evil doers.

The governor, second governor, third governor, and fourth governor carry batons as insignia of office. The baton of the governor is approximately thirty-two inches long, while those of the first three assistant governors are approximately twenty-six inches long. Each of them has a silver head on one end and an iron point on the other. The purpose of the point is to enable the governor or assistant governors to stick the baton in the ground. When during Lent one of these officials arrives at the council house for any official purpose he sticks his baton in the ground before the little wooden cross in front of the council house. When one sees the batons of the governors thus sticking in the ground, he knows that some governmental affairs are in progress.

Each village has a council which deliberates upon policies of community concern. It is a loosely constituted group. The Yaquis themselves are scarcely aware of its existence. When we asked one of them whether each village had a council we usually got a negative answer. Observation convinced us, however, that all matters of a deliberative nature are discussed by the mature men of influence at the council house until a general agreement is reached. Sometimes the discussion may last for days. There is no definite organization except that the governor directs the discussion. The extent to which each man participates is usually in direct proportion to his influence. It is customary for the old men to talk and the young men to listen. We never heard a young man under thirty speak out in council meeting. The young men are always there, but they keep at a respectful distance on the out-' skirts of the group. The average Yaqui puts in more time at the council house than anywhere else, barring the time he spends at home. If there is anything to deliberate upon he either talks and spits or listens and spits. If there is not anything to deliberate about, he merely spits.

The governor and assistant governors constitute a court with jurisdiction over all cases, civil and criminal, except murder. Civil cases pertain mostly to probate matters, questions on boundaries and ownership, and domestic differences. Criminal cases consist for the most part of thievery and of intoxication during the period of Lent. Intoxication during the rest of the year is not considered a crime, and is even regarded by some as an obligation. Fighting, as long as only fists are used, is considered a private matter and no notice is taken of it. In case of thievery the accused is brought before the governors. They investigate to ascertain whether or not he is guilty. If it is the first offense of the accused, he is made to return the goods. If it is the second offense of the accused, he is made to return the goods and is given six lashes by the fifth governor. For each additional offense he is given six lashes. If the culprit is penitent and prays to God for forgiveness, some of the lashes may be remitted. If the thief has already disposed of the stolen goods he is made to pay the rightful owner the value of the goods as determined by the governors and is given lashes according to what offense it is.

Plate 1 - Courtesy of the Texas Archaeological and Paleontological Society.
1. The plumed dancers clan.
2. A Yaqui ceremony, naked Indian represents the Christus.
3. Yaqui funeral, devil-chaser in the foreground.

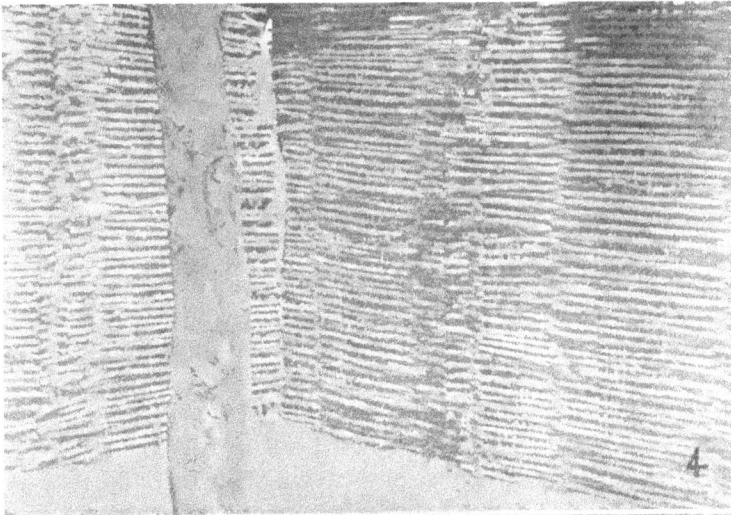

Plate 2 - Courtesy of the Texas Archaeological and Paleontological Society.
4. Interior of Yaqui rooms showing horizontal bamboo weave.
5. A Yaqui kitchen.
6. An arbor in front of a Yaqui house.

Before the fifth governor begins lashing a wrongdoer he has the offender remove his shirt. The fifth governor makes the sign of the cross on his back and then lays on the whip. When the lashing is over a ceremonial question is asked the one who has been punished:

"Why have you been beaten?"

"Because I have stolen a horse." (Or whatever it was.)

'Whose fault is it?"

"My fault."

We were told that it is rare for a person to commit a second offense.

The Yaquis have no jails. Incarceration is not their idea of punishment. In fact, they have only three forms of punishment, — admonition, lashing, and death.

All the Yaqui villages have a central governmental organization in the form of (1) a council and (2) a chief. The council is a primary convention and is as purely democratic as the primary conventions of Switzerland. It is composed of every man and woman of the eight traditional villages. They do not all attend, but it is their privilege to go. The council convenes at irregular intervals for two purposes, (1) to elect a chief or (2) to act as a court to try capital offenses. It has been customary, as long as the oldest men can remember, for the council to meet at Vicam, which is the most centrally located village. When occasion for a meeting arises, word is sent to all the villages for the people to meet at Vicam on a specified date. Those in the outlying villages leave home the day before. The most of them, men, women, children, and dogs, go on foot along trails ankle deep in dust. A few ride horseback. They all carry sufficient food to last several days. It will probably be needed before the convention is over.

If it is the purpose of the council to elect a chief, the governors of the various villages form a caucus. They go over the available men for the position until they find someone on whom they can all agree. This stage of the selection amounts practically to a unanimous agreement. Then the governors go to the delegations from their respective villages and ask for approval of the choice. No vote is taken. If any person opposes the candidate he says so. If there is no opposition, the governor reports to the caucus that his people are agreeable. If no opposition comes from any of the villages, the caucus waits on the one selected and informs him that he is the choice of the people for chief of the eight villages. It is customary for him to decline the position. This disinclination may be sincere or it may be in some cases a mere matter of form. The members of the caucus reason with him until he accepts. There is no side-stepping the will of the people among the Yaquis. The term of office is for life. The average chief is in his fifties or sixties when elected. Unless he is captured or killed by the Mexicans, as has been the case, his term usually lasts for ten to twenty years.

At the present time there is a dual chieftainship which is confusing even to the Yaquis themselves. The real chief is Louis Matos who is now in his seven-

14

ties and who has held the office for twenty years. For the past five years he has been in the mountains, a fugitive from the Mexican government. He refused to be reconstructed and accept the present status of the village Yaquis. He is still regarded as the lawful chief by a large majority of the people in the villages.

The Mexican government, at the time Matos was driven into the mountains because he would not conform to the terms of the treaty of 1929, arbitrarily designated Pluma Blanca of Consica as chief of the Yaquis. Up to that time he had been a minor official in the village of Consica. His selection by the government was due to his pro-Mexican leanings and to the fact that he spoke Spanish fairly well. All government dealings are through Pluma Blanca. The Yaquis do not recognize him except as a matter of convenience in their negotiations with the government.

The second function of the council is judicial. When a capital crime is committed the chief sends runners to all the villages asking the people to assemble at Vicam. A crime is considered as such only when perpetrated by one Yaqui against another Yaqui. The chief presides and all the people, men and women, constitute the jury. The accused may speak for himself or select someone to speak for him. During the trial his hands and feet are tied, and he is kept under guard. The verdict is reached by a sort of mass agreement. With a less orderly procedure it would be called mob agreement. Within the memories of the old men still living, no mass jury has ever failed to convict a person accused of murder. The penalty in such a case is death.

Yaqui justice is as swift as it is sure. There are no appeals, no reversals, no delays, no legal stallings, no jailbreaks, and no escapes. The sentence is carried out the next morning after the verdict is reached. The night before the execution is devoted to the condemned man's funeral. He has the compensating satisfaction of witnessing his own funeral, or the most of it at least. From the time the sentence is pronounced he is treated as a dead person. The devil-chasers mount guard over him and keep the evil spirits away. Chants and prayers are said, the people feast, and fire crackers are shot. One of the most impressive parts of the ceremony is a collection taken up for the condemned man's family. A tin plate is placed before the altar in the church, and while the accused looks on, the people file past and drop in money for the widow, or for his mother, as the case may be. In the morning he is placed before the large cross in front of the church at Vicam, and promptly at eight o'clock a firing squad fires. The lieutenant then goes forward and shoots the fallen man through the head with his pistol. The funeral ceremony is already over except the actual burial which requires but a few minutes. He is covered up and the people are dispersing before he is cold. [2]

Yaqui trials for capital crimes are becoming more and more rare in the river villages. There have been few within the past five years. When such a crime is committed now, the Mexican army officers, if they learn of it, attempt to have the accused apprehended and tried under Mexican law. Governor Miranda of Torin, however, told us that the Yaquis will try desperately to keep the affair concealed from the Mexican military in order that they may try the case according to their ancient custom. The mountain Yaquis still continue tribal judicial procedure without Mexican interference.

The Yaquis pay no taxes to the Mexican government; nor do they levy any local taxes upon themselves. Community enterprises, such as *fiestas* or collections for charity, are financed by free will offerings. The payment of taxes is not included among the worries of the Yaqui. We were told that there is no word for taxation in the Yaqui language.

Military

Under Mexican influence the military society no doubt has undergone a change. The village war chief has been replaced by a *capitan,* a *teniente,* sargeants, and corporals. The warriors are now *soldados.* The most of the members of this society technically belong to the Mexican army; some, however, are not paid by the Mexican government because they did not sign the government rolls at the time of the treaty. On the other hand there are men, not in this organization, who receive pay. The average man of the society going about his everyday routine is a walking arsenal. Around his waist is a cartridge belt filled with cartridges. At his hip hangs a cocked semi-automatic pistol. Inside his belt behind his left hip is a long knife used both for hunting and for *hombres.* Over his right shoulder hangs a repeating rifle which may range anywhere from a 30-30 to 45 calibre. Most of his arms are of American make. The military society never drills. Its main function, it seems, is to march in the numerous funeral and religious processions.

Religious

Most spectacular on ceremonial occasions is the devil-chasers' society. [3] We gave them the name because it so aptly describes their functions. They call themselves the *Fariseos.* Such a name attests to the adaptability of the early padres. They found the devil-chasing organizations among the Yaquis, and being unable to abolish the orders, took them over and made them actors in the miracle plays, which to the Indians became synonymous with Christianity. Their business in pre-Columbian, pagan days was to chase devils, and so it is today.

Mexican influence has been felt in the organization of the devil-chasers' society. At the head is a *capitan,* more generally known as "*el jefe*". As a badge of office he carries a spear. Next in order comes a *teniente,* who has a horsehair rope over his shoulder, and he carries a sword with the point upward. He is followed by four *cabos* (corporals) who have wooden swords which they carry point downward. Next come a flutist and a drummer. These are followed by devil-chasers whose status is comparable to that of privates. Of great importance is another official without military title, *Pilato.* Because of his dress — and the role he played, he is sometimes called Death, a part he represented, no doubt, before the Spaniards came. Membership is optional, yet "once a member always a member." Men usually join the society in fulfillment of a vow taken in some crisiis. For instance, if a Yaqui is deathly sick, he promises God that if he be permitted to get well he will join the devil-chasers. If he does recover, he assumes that God has accepted his offer, and becomes a devil-chaser. [4]

Closely associated with the devil-chasers are the *caballeros,* another religious society. There were eleven of them at Torin; however, they have no fixed number. Their chief is a *capitan* and for a badge of office he carries a large wooden sword; there are three *cabos* with wooden swords, and five knights with wooden lances. The officers ride horses in the processions while the knights walk. The officers are elected for life by the society. Membership in the society is acquired in the same way as in the devil-chasers.

The group called *matachines,* or plume-dancers, is a religious society. In personnel, organization and activity, it has been little influenced by Christian, Spanish, or Mexican influence. The organization is under the sole direction of a *monoja,* or chief. Membership is for life and is acquired when the boys are very young, often as babies. If a boy becomes seriously ill, for instance, his mother promises him to the *matachines* if God permits him to live. There are fourteen members in the society at Torin, their ages ranging from nine to seventy. They wear on their heads tall coronas from the top of which flow colored paper streamers. These no doubt were once feathers of brilliant hues. In their right hands they carry gourd rattles and in their left plumes of chicken feathers. These were in ancient times parrot feathers, perhaps.

Another group of dancers is the *pascolas.* Their organization is loose, and membership is optional. Individuals join or withdraw when they wish. The group is composed of three or four dancers and a half dozen musicians. A deer-dancer is usually associated with them. Unlike the *matachines,* the chief function of the *pascolas* is to entertain. They alternate dancing with "wise-cracking" at funerals, religious *fiestas,* wedding *fiestas,* and christening *fiestas.*

Associated with the church are three societies usually found in a Catholic parish, one for men, and two for women. The men's order, the Society of Saint Ignatius, is headed by a *gobernador,* or beadle. Saint Ignatius is the patron saint of Torin. There are three *maestros* who conduct services when the regular Catholic priest is not present. This is most of the time as the priest comes through only once or twice a year. Next is the *sacristan,* or *temachi,* who rings the bells, lights candles, and acts as head janitor. He is assisted by two or three understudies. Several altar boys comprise the remainder of the group.

The older women have a society called in Yaqui *qui yoste.* It is the Society of the Virgin of Loretta or the Society of Our Lady of Loretta. The group cares

17

for the images, does various tasks, usually done by women's church societies, and carries images of the saints in the numerous processions.

The younger women and girls have a society known as the "Children of Mary". They assist at work around the church, prepare for the various services, and take orders generally from the older women. On one occasion in the *Fiesta de Gloria* they carry the image of Mary in her search for the risen Jesus.

The choir can scarcely be said to be an organization. It is composed of any number of women, and is closely associated with the *maestros.* They sing the responses and chants for all services.

All the seven last named organizations have to do more or less with religion. In fact, the Yaquis are extremely religious. They do everything religiously, even their drinking. When they shoot Mexicans, they do it religiously. A considerable part of their time is devoted to religious activities. Their religion is a mixture of Catholicism and paganism, a Christian theme largely observed with pagan ritual. Their churches combine the elements of Christian temple and pagan shrine. They are made of poles and *carrizo* somewhat after the manner of our old-fashioned brush arbors. The services are conducted almost entirely by the beadle and the maestros. These wear no vestments, but dress in blue denim and sandals like the other men. Training for these positions is got by the apprentice method. The *maestros* do no preaching, but lead the endless prayers and chants.

Religious observances consist for the most part of pageantry and miracle plays. The Yaquis possess a keen sense of the dramatic. Their religious *fiestas* consist of a series of dramatic episodes in which Biblical and pagan characters are impersonated. They observe six general *fiestas* in the course of the year and one local *fiesta* in honor of the individual saint of each village. Of the general *fiestas,* the eve of Saint John's Day is given over to social festivities, and Saint John's Day proper, June 24, to religious ceremonies. Saint Francis' Day on September 24 is observed with religious processions and services. A similar observance takes place the day of the Conception on December 8, and another on the Day of the Virgin of Guadalupe, December 12. The celebration of Christmas lasts a week. The most important of all is the *Fiesta de Gloria* at Easter.

During the observance of Lent, Yaquis observe an impressive ceremony each evening just at dusk. A drummer goes out from the council house of each village, stands before the cross in front of the council house, and beats a continuous roll for several minutes. Then he faces in each of the four directions making a sort of curtsy by placing the toe of one foot just behind the heel of the other. While he is beating the drum all men within hearing place their hats on the ground in front of them and stand at attention facing the drummer until the ceremony is over. The Yaquis explained to us that this was a sort of silent prayer. Since the use of the drum and the facing in four directions are pagan practices we surmised that the early Catholic missionaries took over an ancient native ceremony and adapted it as a sort of vesper service. Yaquis observe certain Christian practices of fasting. They never eat meat on Friday; and during Holy Week they eat no meat on Wednesday, Thursday, or Friday.

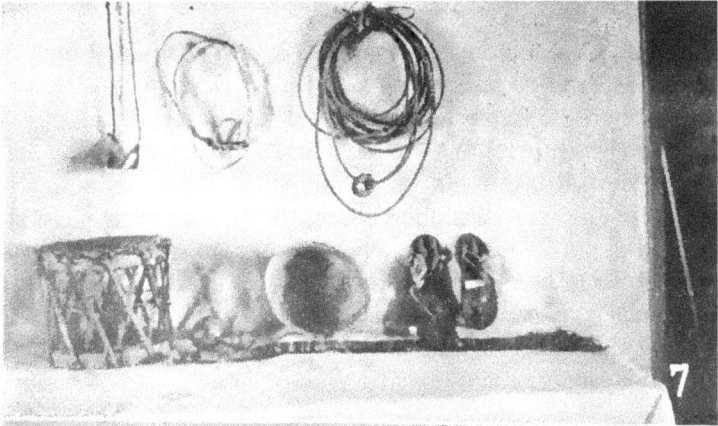

Plate 3 - Courtesy of the Texas Archaeological and Paleontological Society.
7. Yaqui slingshot, rawhide thong for wood carrying, rawhide lariat, stool, gourd
nursing bottle, tortilla basket, sandals, whisk broom and sash
8. Yaqui musical instruments.
9. Cooking utensils, two wooden spoons, wooden bowl, and earthen cooking pot.

A widespread belief in ghosts prevails among the Yaquis. Practically every adult person has had one or more "experiences" with a ghost. These "experiences" are not hard to come by, for the men especially, as the most of them imbibe more or less mescal from time to time. The most realistic ghost story we got was from the old *temachi*, or bell-ringer at the church. One night when he was at the church alone ringing the bell about 9 o'clock, a ghost came out of the church, passed near him, walked out about fifty yards, and sat down on a rock. The old *temachi* got a good view of him as he passed. He wore a long, black robe or coat. He had a very large, white head, and a flat face. When we asked the old man how long the ghost sat on the rock, he said he did not stay to see.

[1] It is to be remembered that the Yaqui makes no differentiation in governmental functions. To him the governor is an elected chief. He often refers to the governor and assistant governors as "los jefes" (the chiefs). In short the Yaqui makes only one classification in the functions of government wherein we make several. It is for the purpose of analysis that I apply our governmental terminology to the Yaqui system. The Yaqui himself would be confused by it.

[2] The following account of a Yaqui murder trial was given us by a Mexican who claimed that it was told to him by an old Yaqui woman. We were unable to get the story verified by any of the old Yaqui men, but it is worth repeating. One Yaqui killed another. The murderer was arrested and tried by the general council of all the villages and found guilty. But the execution, instead of following the usual custom, was postponed for eight days. During this time the condemned one was given the best food and everything else that he wanted. Each day the people took him to church and prayed for his soul. On the last night his funeral service was held. Early on the morning of the eighth day he was taken to the cemetery where he witnessed the digging of his grave. At eight o'clock he was placed before the large cross in front of the church and shot by eight soldiers with eight bullets. The shooting was officially watched by eight women, madrinas. There were one bullet and one woman for each of the eight villages. Then the body was buried by the women.

[3] The Yaqui word for devil-chaser is chapayecam.

[4] For an account of the dress of various members of the devil-chasers' society, see chapter on Fiesta de Gloria.

Ralph L. Beals in collaboration with Elsie Clews Parsons in an article, "The Sacred Clowns of the Pueblo and Mayo-Yaqui Indians", *American Anthropologist,* Vol. 36, No. 4, October-December, 1934, gives a more detailed account of the devil-chasers.

Chapter Two - Marriage, Child Rearing, and Education

William Curry Holden

Marriage

The initiative in marriage negotiations rests in theory with the mother of the boy. Considerable freedom is allowed young people before marriage, and matches are often the result of understandings between the boy and girl in question. But it is for the mother of the boy to make the first public move. The degree to which a mother follows the wishes of her son as to choice of the girl depends upon the dominating nature of the mother and the acquiescing nature of the son. Qualities in their prospective daughters-in-law which all Yaqui mothers rate foremost are health, vitality, robustness, and industry. The most desirable girl is heavy set, strong limbed and strong backed, large hipped, and heavy breasted. Such physical qualities are almost indispensable to fit the bride for the strenuous life of a Yaqui wife and mother. The slender, American, boyish type of girl would never be selected by a Yaqui mother.

Theoretically, the mother takes the step in match-making by first deciding on a girl and then taking the matter up with her son and husband. If all these parties are favorable, the boy's mother makes a date with the parents of the girl to discuss the matter. The meeting of the four parents takes place at the home of the girl. The visiting parents ask for the girl for their daughter, saying they will treat her well and respect her. If the girl's parents object to the match they veto the proposal, and that is the end of it unless there is a tremendous infatuation between the young couple. Their only recourse is to run away and begin living together in a common law relationship, a thing which is occasionally done. The usual rule is, however, for the girl's parents to agree. The engagement is manifested by the boy's presenting the girl with a wedding dress. This is usually made by his mother and sisters.

The wedding takes place at the Yaqui church the next time the priest comes through. Inasmuch as he comes only once or twice a year, there may be several weddings at the same time. The ceremony takes place between eight and nine in the morning. It is the usual Catholic ceremony. After it is over the Yaqui *maestro* draws the couple aside and gives them advise. He tells them to love each other, to be faithful, and to respect their parents. Then he gives special allegorical admonitions to the boy. The world is full of pitfalls. First, he must avoid water (the evils of drink); second, he must beware of iron (not indulge in needless fighting); and third, he must shun darkness (not stray from the good faith). In addition he tells the girl not to look to the right or the left when she goes out, for the devil is lurking about and will tempt her. Failure to observe any of the above admonitions will bring unhappiness. The bride and bridegroom swear to heed the advice by the holy cross which they make with thumb and forefinger.

The newlyweds, with their families and friends, then proceed to the home of the boy's parents where preparations have been made for an all-day *fiesta*. The bride wears the wedding dress until noon, when she takes it off and puts it away. It is kept until her death. If she has not grown too stout, it is her burial gown. If she is too large for it, it is rolled into a bundle and placed under her head "so that God can see what she was married in." After she takes off her wedding dress on her wedding day, the bride helps with the cooking and serving of food for the assembled crowd, — beans, *tortillas*, stew of wild meat, and black, vile coffee. The musicians and *pascolas* are there to dance. There is plenty of mescal. Most of the men and boys partake of it in varying amounts. Some of them will become thoroughly drunk. There may be quarrels and fist fights. The party breaks up in the late afternoon, and the guests able to travel go home. Those who have become completely intoxicated will lie in the dust in the yard or in the road, depending upon where they happened to fall over, until they regain consciousness in the night or next morning. Then they stagger on home with bleared eyes and bursting heads.

It is customary for the couple to live at the house of the boy's parents. If the boy is enterprizing he has built a new bamboo room near or attached to the house of the family. It is most likely, however, that he has not gone to this trouble. In this case, they are assigned a corner of a room already occupied by several members of the family. There is little privacy in a Yaqui household. The bride assumes her share of the women's work, and begins her monotonous career of grinding corn, cooking *tortillas*, carrying wood and water, and raising babies.

Due to the influence of the Catholic church, monogamy prevails among the Yaquis today. There is little doubt, however, that before the advent among them of Chrisitanity they were polygamists. One evidence of this is to be found in the calmness with which they, religious as they are, view irregular unions of a polygamous character. We shall give an example. Juan Serrano is between forty-five and fifty. He stays drunk most of the time except during a holy *fiesta*. He is very religious, and takes an important part in all religious ceremonies and funerals. His home is a veritable harem. We had occasion to be in his house often and tried to unravel the relationship of his various women. None of them was "his lawfully wedded wife." Thai individual had left him years ago. "She went off with another man". The oldest woman in his harem, whom we shall call wife Number 1, was about the same age as Juan, between forty-five and fifty. She was the lawful wife of a friend of Juan's. The friend had gone to Arizona ten or twelve years before and had "loaned" her to Juan. She had a daughter when Juan "borrowed" her, and she has since had six children by Juan. These children are all girls except the last one, a boy about two years old, whom Juan worships. Wife Number 2 was a young women not over twenty. She had two babies by Juan. The older is dead, and the second, a boy six months old, was sick when we saw it. It probably did not live. Wife Number 3 was the daughter of wife Number 1. She was a full-

22

breasted, sleek-skinned, sensuous girl of sixteen. At the time we were there last she was some eight months advanced with child. There was another young woman in the household, a "cousin" of Number 3, whose position we could not make out, but it is probable that she served as wife Number 4 to Juan. All the women lived together in harmony and amicability under the supervision of the oldest one.

Juan's polygamy is tolerated by the community. There is no doubt a certain amount of gossip going around, but neither Juan nor any of his numerous family are ostracized socially. All of the various wives participate in the religious and social life of the village; a condition which indicates to some degree that the Yaqui people have traditionally been accustomed to plural wives.

The Yaquis are much more exacting in their rules pertaining to exogamy than to those relating to monogamy. Public opinion does not permit incest. There is no evidence today that exogamy among them is based on any kind of clan system, as is the case with other American Indian tribes. If such were ever the case the practice has been dropped. No one can marry his blood kin. The degree to which prohibitions are placed upon blood relationships is vague. It evidently extends beyond first cousins. The practice of incest is looked upon as very low and beastly. Any one guilty of it is regarded as an animal, and superstition has it that he may even turn into an animal. He has the same political status as an outlaw has in our country, — one outside of the law, and it is no crime for any citizen to kill him.

Interracial marriages are opposed by the Yaquis. Their opposition to intermarrying with the Mexicans is augmented to some extent by racial hatred but it is basically religious. They look with disfavor upon their young people's marrying Anglo-Americans. They believe that the Yaquis will be segregated in heaven, and if one marries outside the tribe he will be separated from his people in the next world. In the villages where the social practices are still regulated by tribal tradition and opinion there is practically no intermarrying with the Mexicans. The force of tribal customs breaks down, however, when young men leave the villages to work in Mexican or American communities. A Yaqui youth on a ranch in northern Sonora is likely to marry a Mexican girl. If he does he is lost to the tribe and is absorbed into the Mexican race. We could find no instance where a young man had returned to the villages bringing a Mexican wife with him.

Divorce theoretically does not exist among the Yaquis, but in reality it is quite prevalent. Here again we find the ancient customs of the people hanging on in sharp conflict with the more recent mandates of the Catholic church. As in most other American Indian tribes, divorce no doubt was easy among the Yaquis prior to the seventeenth century. Then came the padres with their teaching of monogamy and no divorces. Today a Yaqui cannot obtain, either from the tribal authorities or otherwise, a lawful divorce. But the church does not prohibit a man or woman from forsaking his or her lawful spouse and taking up with another. Our inquiry indicated that at least fifteen percent of the adults having families are now living under such conditions. No social stigma is attached to the practice, and the children are christened by the church without any questions as to their legitimate status.

The Yaquis are quite frank in their conversation on matters pertaining to sex. Both men and women answered questions and volunteered comments without embarrassment in the presence of their families and neighbors. Sex relations is common among unmarried people and adultery to some extent among married persons. If the relations of young unmarried persons become known, they are given a good lecture by the old people. Such reproof is a matter of form and is not taken too seriously. Women seemed to be more unfaithful than men and with physiological cause, perhaps. From all appearances, Yaqui women as a whole are highly sexed. We were told there are a few "professional" prostitutes among them. The customary price is a *peso,* or a piece of cheap jewelry, or a dress. Such women are the object of considerable gossip, but are not socially ostracized.

Child Rearing

Yaquis love children. They simply cannot have too many. Because of the high infant mortality rate they must bring many of them into the world in order to have a few reach maturity. The bearing of children is the main interest and pleasure of a Yaqui woman. With her, pregnancy is a pleasure because she experiences its stimulating and exalting effects and little of the nausea and illness so common with white women.

Pregnancy is a condition of which Yaqui women are not ashamed. On the contrary they are proud of it. They laugh and make jokes about it with their friends and neighbors, men as well as women. The only precautions which a Yaqui woman seems to take while carrying a child is in not lifting heavy objects. Delivery requires from three hours to three days, the most of the cases being less than six hours. Caesarian operations are unknown to them. If a mother is not delivered in the natural way she dies. Little trouble is encountered in childbirth by Yaqui women, however, as they characteristically have large pelvic areas and unusual vitality. As a rule a woman is attended in delivery by a midwife only. In some cases the medicine man gives the assistance. Occasionally women wait on themselves. We talked with one woman who had had three children. With two of them she waited entirely on herself. In one case she had cut the cord too short and the child bled to death. The woman is usually in a kneeling position when the birth occurs. The placenta comes out promptly, seldom longer than fifteen minutes after the birth. It is buried in ashes or placed in the top of a tree, for Yaquis believe that if it is not disposed of properly it will cause trouble when the next child is born. The mother usually rests on a mat from two to five days. Then she gets up and goes about her duties. A few women never go to bed at all. However, they all observe a forty day period of ceremonial purification.

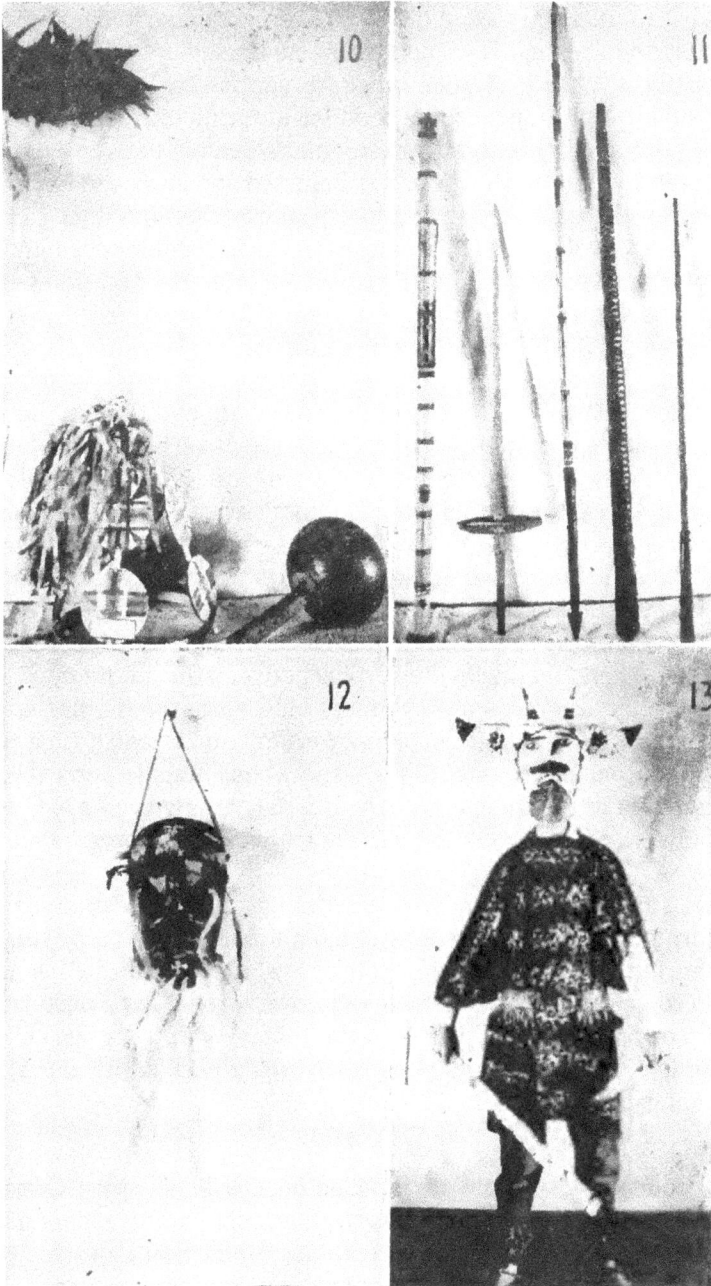

Plate 4 - Courtesy of the Texas Archaeological and Paleontological Society.
10. Plume, corona, and gourd rattle of a plumed dancer.
11. Left to right, bamboo flute, a whirling device for twisting horse hair into strands, arrow with wooden point, notched music stick, smooth music stick.
12. Deer dancer's mask.
13. Devil-chaser.

The baby, immediately after birth, is given a calendric name, washed in tepid water, and dressed. The calendric name is used until after the christening. The baby is nursed by some other woman for six to seven days, as the mother's milk is not thought to be good for it during this period. Meanwhile, the mother drains her breasts by massaging. When ten to twelve days old the child is taken to the church where it is baptized and christened by the *maestro*. It is given the name of a godfather or godmother, in either case a good friend, *un bueno amigo,* of the parents. After the christening the family with a number of invited guests return home and celebrate the occasion with a fiesta, including a dinner and more or less *mescal*. At the end of the *fiesta* all the guests shake hands with the father three times, congratulating him upon his achievement.

Mothers nurse their children until they are from two to four years of age. We saw one women nursing a child five years old. This custom of nursing children for long durations is one of the saving graces of Yaqui child-rearing and helps to reduce the appallingly high infant mortality rate. The only milk Yaqui children ever get is from their mothers. The women have large breasts which produce an unusual amount of milk. Occasions have been noted where a woman would be nursing a baby a few months old, a child of two, and a child of four, all at the same time. On such occasions the mother would give the baby its fill first and divide the surplus between the other two.

The child is not more than six months old before the mother starts supplementing its milk with mashed beans, *tortilla* crumbs, and even green corn, if in season. "Stomach trouble" follows and a considerable percentage of Yaqui babies die of intestinal disorders before they are two years old. Without a good supply of mother's milk the percentage would no doubt be much higher.

At home Yaqui boys seldom wear clothes up to three or four years of age except during the winter. When away from home at a *fiesta* or church they wear a short, plain dress or a tiny pair of overalls and shirt. Girls are never permitted to go naked. Up to the age of two children wear a peculiar kind of diaper. It consists of a string around the thighs, with a rag which runs between the legs and tucks under the thigh string back and front. The rag is seldom changed.

Education

A boy's education is simple. He is called in occasionally by his parents and given instruction in how to greet people, in respect for his elders or juniors, general conduct, and behavior at ceremonies. Membership in a society is optional. He is taught to hunt with bow and arrow and with a slingshot. He absorbs from his elders a considerable knowledge of woodcraft. The chances are that he will not go to school. Only about one boy out of ten ever learns to read or write. The reason for his illiteracy lies with his elders. The old men are opposed to the Mexican schools. They well know that the best way for the government to break down Yaqui resistance is to get the Yaqui children into Mexican schools, under Mexican teachers. The old men have so far managed to prevent the most of the children's attending school. The government maintains a school in each village but only a handful of Yaqui children ever attend. When asked why they did not send their children to school, fathers gave various reasons. It was too expensive to buy clothes, pencils and paper, or they needed their children at home. Such trumped-up excuses were easy to see through. They feared the Mexicanizing influence of the schools.

At Torin out of a scholastic population of approximately a hundred only eight Yaqui children attend school. The governors agreed to permit these to attend provided a Yaqui man who spoke both Yaqui and Spanish should stay in the school room and translate what the Mexican teacher said into Yaqui. This is a safeguard calculated to offset to some degree the Mexicanizing influence of the school. Consequently, the Yaqui man, without pay, stays as faithfully in the school room as the Mexican teacher.

The training of Yaqui girls is given by their mothers. Education for the main purpose of their lives, child bearing and rearing, begins early. One is scarcely five or six before she is helping to care for a younger member of the family. By the time she is seven she can carry a baby on her back, and balance a two-gallon bucket of water on her head with ease. Long before she is old enough to marry she knows how to carry wood and water, to grind corn into meal, to mix the dough, to pat out and cook *tortillas,* and to beat out clothes at a waterhole in the river.

Yaqui children are shy, reserved, and well behaved. When strangers are about the place, the little ones cling to their mothers, their big dark eyes riveted on the visitors. Small boys who stay constantly in the fields during the growing season to scare away the birds and devastating animals are as shy as their sisters at home. If they see you before you see them they will hide and watch you like a hawk as long as you are in sight. If you come on them unawares they immediately have business on the other side of the field and glide off so easily that they leave you wondering how they did it. One day we were passing a field in a car. A boy some fifty yards from the road had a bow and arrow. We decided to stop and attempt to purchase them. We called to the boy just as he was taking aim at an imaginary rabbit, in the opposite direction. He shot his arrow as far as he could and then ran after it. He shot again in the same direction and chased on after his arrow, — a neat trick, we thought, of getting away from us.

Yaqui parents seem to have a sincere affection for their children. Two instances are typical. One day Dr. Wagner found a baby taking water from a gourd "nursing bottle". The Doctor decided we must have the "bottle" for our museum collection. He offered the mother a half *peso* for it. She refused and said the "bottle" belonged to the baby and she would not sell it. A *peso.* Two *pesos.* No, it belonged to the baby and was not for sale. Then the Doctor changed his tactics and offered brilliantly colored beads and cheap, flashy jewelry which a Yaqui woman finds hard to resist. No, the gourd was the baby's. Then the Doctor dug deeper into his pockets and found a little red automobile. The mother began to soften. She called the baby's father. They held a lengthy consultation. Yaqui words flew fast. They agreed to trade. The baby had rather have the little red automobile than the bottle. The toy had cost the Doctor a dime at a ten cent store. It is to be noted here that the parents put the desires of the baby foremost. They refused two *pesos* for the gourd and took a toy costing ten cents, — all because it would please the baby. This instance also emphasized the fact that the Yaquis are not as yet commercially minded. They have practically no sense of monetary values. While securing museum specimens we found they usually took whatever we offered for an object. If they were willing to part with an item, the price was not a consideration. They would sell a rawhide covered stool for fifty *centavos* as readily as for five *pesos*.

A second instance of fondness for children was noted at the home of the village carpenter at Torin, The carpenter made stools and chairs which he traded to his neighbors for corn, beans and melons. For his grandchildren he had made a tiny chair, a crib for the baby to stand in, and a little wagon. The carpenter was wi 1ing to sell us anything else on the place including his ceremonial plume and headgear, for he was a member of the *matachines,* but the children's things were not for sale,

Le:s than ten percent of Yaqui men can read, and the number of women is even smaller. We visited in some fifty homes and in only one did we find any kind of newspaper. This was in the house of Lorenzo Espinosa, the most respected and influential man in Vicam. There we found a dozen copies of the *Excelsior,* of widely varying dates. From these Lorenzo gathered news of political activities in Mexico. These items he told to his neighbors and they in turn relayed them on until the news spread through the different villages. Consequently, even illiterate Yaquis have some idea of political trends in the nation.

Chapter Three - La Fiesta De Gloria

William Curry Holden

La Fiesta de Gloria is the longest and most important of Yaqui ceremonies. It is the culmination of a series of observances held throughout Lent. The ceremony upon which this account is based was witnessed at Torin. [1] Beginning at eight o'clock on Wednesday evening before Easter it lasts until noon Sunday. Separate ceremonies are held in each of the five river villages including Vicam "Switch". We were unable to learn whether the Yaquis in the mountains observed *La Gloria* with a complete ceremonial. It seemed customary for some of the mountain Yaquis to slip down to the river villages for the celebration.

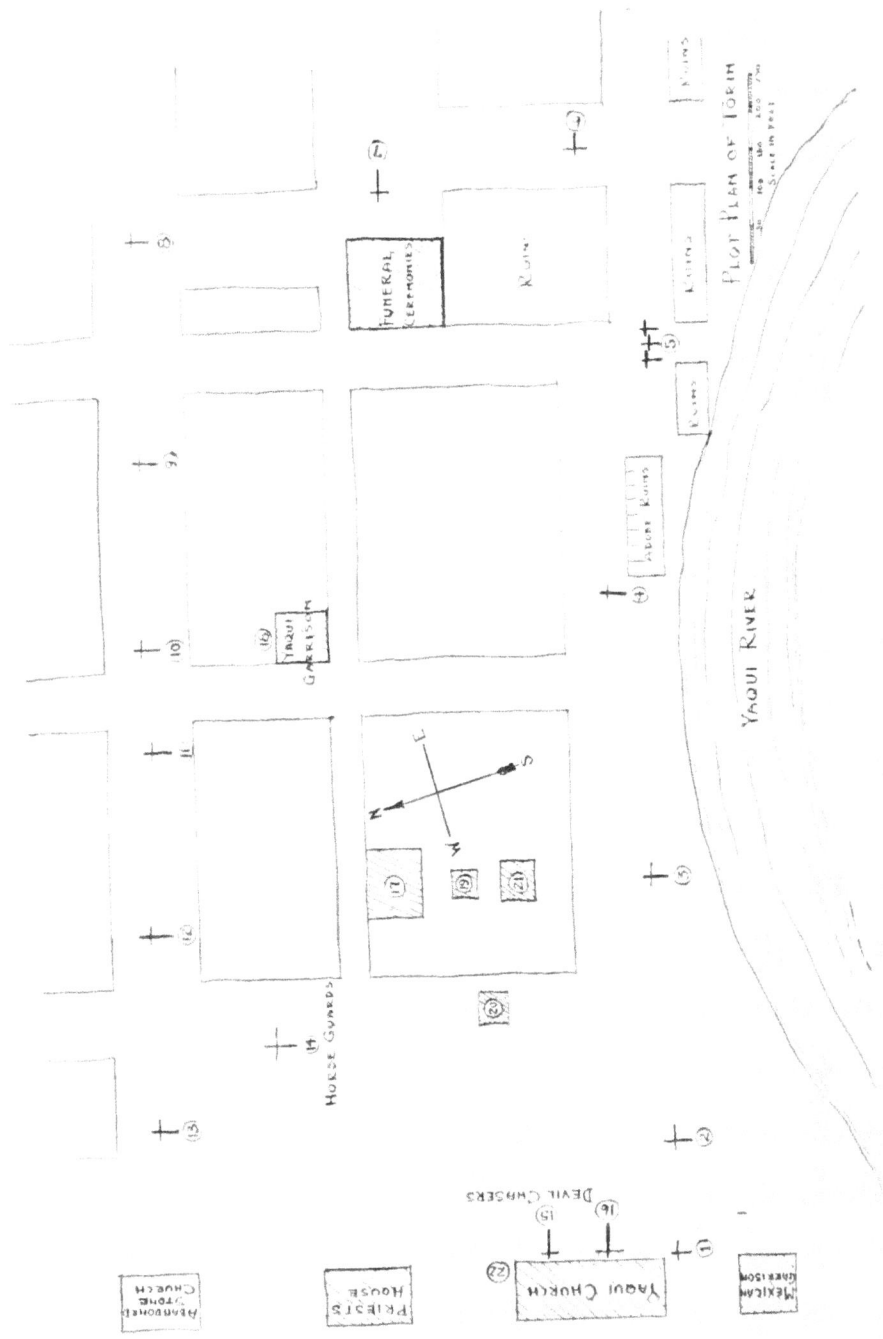

PLOT PLAN OF TÓRIM

YAQUI RIVER

FUNERAL CEREMONIES

RUINS

ALDEA ROAD

YAQUI GARRISON

HORSE GUARDS

DEVIL CHASERS

YAQUI CHURCH

PRIESTS HOUSE

ABANDONED STONE CHURCH

MEXICAN GARRISON

Plate 5

The preparations for the *Fiesta* at Torin were under the direction of a *Jefe de la Fiesta,* who on this occasion was the chief of the devil-chasers' clan. On Tuesday and Wednesday members of the devil-chasers' organization built an inclosure of bamboo cane some fifty feet square surrounding a huge tree (SI 7, Plate 5). The sides of the inclosure were from twelve to fifteen feet high, affording a very good wind-break. The entrance was on the south side. The tree shaded most of the area which was used for cooking. Women, children, and dogs were grouped about a half dozen fires which were kept going continuously during the entire time. Each day several young men detailed for the purpose brought in huge wagon loads of seasoned mesquite wood for fuel.

Throughout Wednesday people were coming in from the country. Practically all of them came on foot, the women carrying on their heads the food they would need during the next four days. They camped under trees or among the ruined walls of Torin. A few families made wind-breaks of cottonwood boughs. They needed to spend little time preparing their camps,

Plot of the village of Torin. The crosses on the plot indicate stations at which ceremonies was held. These are referred to in the text as S1, S2, and so on.

however, for they would be in them very little. The men would be at their respective society's headquarters and the women would divide their time between the church, marching in the numerous processions, and the cooking inclosure. Sleep and rest would be had in snatches when and where a lull came in the festivities.

In order to observe every phase of the ceremonies we divided our party into four shifts, two persons to the shift. Working in two and one-half hour watches day and night we took notes and recorded the time at which everything took place. In order not to make this report too long and monotonous we shall omit a considerable part of the detail contained in the notes. Should anyone desire to make a future study of the *Fiesta de Gloria* and wish to draw a comparison, our field notes will be on file.

The *fiesta* was officially started with the beating of a drum in front of the Yaqui garrison (S18, Plate 5) at 8:00 o'clock Wednesday evening. Fifteen minutes later two candles were lighted on the altar of the church, and after another five minutes a third and fourth candle were lighted, giving the altar a stage effect. At 8:25 the bells of the church were rung, and at the same time a drum was beaten at the Yaqui garrison. The drum sounded again at 8:43 and the military society formed in front of the garrison in a column of twos. These men marched to the church, entering from the south, stood for a moment crossing themselves, marched out again and around the church to the northeast corner, where they built a fire at S22. This station remained the civil and military societies' headquarters until the end of the fiesta.

The devil-chasers had planted their banner (a small red flag with a white cross on it) at S15 in the afternoon. Throughout the late afternoon and early evening the members had been arriving with their paraphernalia under their arms. They planted their wooden swords in the ground around the banner and placed their masks on the swords. The evening was cool, and they started a fire. The ringing of the church bells at 8:50 was the signal for every devil-chaser to put on his paraphernalia — a blanket with a slit in it for the head, a deer-hoof belt to confine it at the waist, and cocoon-rattler anklets. [2] Each man threw himself prone upon the ground on his left side to put on his mask. This is customary for putting on and removing masks. Each devil-chaser wears a small wooden cross swung from his neck. Just before he pulls his mask over his head he places the cross in his mouth where it remains until he removes the mask. During this time he does not utter a word. He communicates entirely by signals. Belonging to the devil-chaser society were ten members who wore black veils over their heads and shoulders and who carried either painted wooden swords or spears. These men were of higher rank than the ordinary devil-chasers. If the latter might be compared to privates in the army, the black-masked marvels would be as corporals or sergeants. The dress of one of the black marvels was more elaborate than the others. He was a tall man and wore a black felt hat. A black veil reaching to the shoulders covered his head. From his shoulders to his knees hung a long black cape edged with yellow braid. This man, an imposing and dramatic figure, was to impersonate Pilate, King Herod, Danger, and Death successively in the course of the evening ceremonies.

The devil-chaser society formed into a column of twos. Fire works were shot off at 9:27, and at 9:30 the clan started to the church, marching to the tune of a bamboo flute. Entering the church, the two lines separated, one going on the east side and one on the west. Women and children had been arriving in small groups for an hour. They sat flat on the ground in the center of the church. Presently the governor, with the other three chiefs and the military clan, returned and stood in three columns in the rear of the church.

The next forty minutes were consumed in taking up a collection. A bamboo mat with a blanket on it was placed in front of the altar. On the blanket was a pottery plate. On each side, reclining on his elbows, was a devil-chaser. One had a stuffed bird, the other a stuffed squirrel. Apparently the bird and squirrel took a great interest in the collection. They would look into the plate and wag their heads in disappointment at the small amount of money coming in. The contributors came in pairs, knelt before the plate, crossed themselves, and made their offering. Most of the men gave a peso; the women and children gave less. When no more seemed forthcoming five men gathered around the mat to count the money. When they had finished, one of them, an old man, stood up and made a speech, He spoke in Yaqui, but we gathered that he was talking about the collection. When he finally dramatically announced the amount, 78 *pesos,* a chorus of Yaqui "Amens" arose from the audience. An unusual amount it seemed; it was to be used to pay the expenses of the *fiesta.* They would use hundreds of candles, a quantity of flour and corn meal, and two old steers that had been purchased for meat.

The mat was removed at 10:15, and a lay assistant to the priest (known as *maestro*) began lighting candles on a special candlestick in front of the altar. The *maestro* and women started a chant and the devil-chasers gathered around the altar beating time with their wooden swords. For the next hour and forty-five minutes chants and prayers alternated with the devil-chasers' beating their sticks and an occasional drum-beat, with a few notes on the flute. At 10:48 a *maestro* extinguished one of the candles. At three to five minute intervals the other candles were put out one at a time.

At 11:48 the church was in total darkness. Then came a whipping ceremony. It started with someone's crowing like a rooster. Men and women pulled their skirts up over their backs. For seven minutes bedlam reigned. Worshippers whipped one another on the bare backs with straps. They yelled, shrieked, cried, laughed, and screamed. The fat woman who led the chorus beat the *maestro* lustily. At 11:55 candles were re-lighted. The people knelt for a final prayer and the service was over. Exactly at midnight the devil-chasers left* followed by the governor's staff and military society. As the people left the church they bellowed like calves, barked like dogs, or screeched like owls. The candles were allowed to burn out one by one. The last one flickered out at 12:35. The people spent the rest of the night lounging, some of them sleeping, around their camp fires.

Activities were started Thursday morning at 5:55 with the ringing of the church bells, eight slow, deep strokes followed by a series of chimes. At 6:15 drumbeats came from the Yaqui garrison. At S15 and S14 respectively, where they had spent the latter part of the night, were the devil-chasers and the mounted guard. The latter had their standard planted under a huge tree. Only eight of them, the older men, were actually mounted; horses not in use were tied under the tree.

Between seven and eight women carried breakfast to the men of the various groups. It consisted of *tortillas* and coffee. At 8:10 the drum at the Yaqui garrison was beaten again.

Several women gathered at the church. Some of them began sweeping the dirt floor with brush brooms. Others were carrying water in five-gallon cans on their heads from the waterholes in the river. They sprinkled the floor and moistened the tops of the graves.

At 8:42 a group of ten persons, eight of them women, arrived with a corpse of a baby, which had died the night before of pneumonia. (See funeral number 4 in the chapter on funerals.) At 8:55 the bell ringer tolled the bells for the funeral. While the grave was being dug and the other details cared for, no one took any notice of the funeral except the little group which had come with the body. Women kept on sweeping a few yards away; the devil-chasers were sprawled on the ground nearby; many persons came and went as unconcerned as if there were no funeral within a hundred miles.

In the meanwhile there was considerable bustle and activity throughout the entire village. Two members of the military society were sweeping the area around the Yaqui garrison with huge brush brooms, causing clouds of dust to rise. Men and women were cleaning the space around the cooking shelter at S17. Smoke was rising from piles of burning trash. Several men were building a bamboo arbor, some fourteen feet square, at S19. This was to be used later in the day for a ceremonial feast. Women in the compound at S17 had never stopped cooking, and throughout the morning they were busy preparing an unusual variety of foods.

At 10:20 the *maestros* and the singers led by a very fat woman whom we called "old High Pitch" started a chant in the church, old High Pitch's voice drowning out the voices of the other women. Ten minutes later the devil-chasers gathered at S15 and began putting on their masks. At 10:37 a drum sounded and the devil-chasers formed a double line. At 10:38 they began their march to the church to the music of a flute, beating together their wooden swords. Shortly before them, the governor's staff had arrived and taken up their position in three lines near the rear of the church. The governor's staff consisted of the assistant governors and all ex-governors and ex-assistant governors. When the devil-chasers arrived the two lines spread out, passed outside the governor's staff, and went near the front of the church. The governor and the first three assistant governors, with blue sashes around their shoulders, then left their places in the rear of the church and went forward and stood to the left of the altar. Before the altar was a statue of Christ surrounded by four sets of candles. The m*aestros* and singers were still chanting, and the devil-chasers beat their swords rhythmically, rattled their anklets and occasionally their deer-hoof belts by shaking their hips. At 10:43, Pilate and the chief of the devil-chasers advanced to the altar, where they stood silently for three minutes; then they returned to their places and the chanting was resumed. At 10:50 the *maestros* and singers knelt for two minutes while the old bell-ringer and his first assistant shook rattling boards near the altar. Each board was about three feet long and twelve inches wide; on each were three or four iron rings about four inches in diameter, each ring attached with a single staple in such a way that it would swing around freely when the board was shaken; at the top of each board was a handhold. When the board was shaken vigorously with a half rotating motion, back and forth, the rings clapped loudly against the board, making a great noise. The purpose of the rattling boards was not clear. While the bell-ringers were shaking the boards and the *maestros* and women were kneeling, the devil-chasers were jumping about, clowning, and making a lot of horseplay.

At 11:00 the clatter stopped, and there was responsive reading by the maestros and singers, the *maestros* reading from prayer-books and the women responding by rote. A silent prayer at 11:04 was followed by a chant which ended at 11:08. The governor and the three assistants left the place where they were standing at the left of the altar and went back to the governor's staff at the rear of the church. At 11:12 the devil-chasers marched out to the accompaniment of flute-playing to the east side of the church where they removed their masks and began to smoke cigarettes and to rest, — but not for long. At 11:20, they put on their masks and scattered out around the village, one taking his place at each of the crosses, stations 1 to 15 inclusive. Then the old bell-ringer brought one of the rattle-boards and gave it to the devil-chaser stationed at S1. The board was carried around the village in relay fashion. When the first board had got to the opposite side of the village the bell-ringer started the second board. Around the village the boards went clanging three times. It was a hot day; the men ran fast; sweat rolled down their necks and saturated their heavy serapes; not a dry thread was left. With their heads encased in tight buckskin masks we wondered why they did not fall from exhaustion, but they did not. They were driving away evil spirits and throwing their protecting influence around the village as their ancestors had done from time immemorial.

Meanwhile, the women who had charge of the ceremonial property were dressing a two-foot statue of Christ in a red robe. Around his neck they placed a horse-hair rope. Then they brought out a three-foot statue of Mary and dressed her in white; the garments had been washed, starched and ironed. A statue of Mary Magdalene, dressed in black, was brought out and placed on the east side of the church towards the front. A crown of thorns was placed on the head of Christ, and the statue was placed upon a litter.

The clapper-board relay ended at 11:40, and nine minutes later a general procession of all the societies got under way. An old man told us they "were going to look for Christ." They were led by Death, alias Herod, who rode a beautiful white horse. The horse's mane and tail were made festive with bows and streamers of colored paper. He had been trained to lope no faster than an ordinary horse can walk. While the societies marched around the village looking for Christ in the red robe, the devil-chaser who remained in the church held the horse-hair rope attached to Christ's neck in one hand and wielded his long wooden sword with the other. He jumped around, shook his hips, and made passes through the air with his sword.

At 11:58 the searchers returned to find Christ at the church and they proceeded to make a great commotion over him. The governor and the first three assistant governors then came forward, picked up the litter on which the Christ rested, and started a new procession. The devil-chaser holding the rope went along in front, still holding the rope fast. Pilate rode in front of the group. By his side, on foot, went one of the black-masked devil-chasers, and behind them, the governors bearing the Christ. Flanking both sides were the members of the military society in columns of twos, each man fully armed. The mounted guardsmen were outside the military columns, three horsemen on either side, each holding erect his wooden spear or sword. The procession went around the village, stopping briefly at each of the fourteen crosses. As they approached S18 they were met by the *maestros* and the singers, who had remained at the church. The Christ was placed where he had been before, the devil-chaser still holding the rope. The singers and the governor's staff knelt for a prayer while the devil-chasers and military guards stood in lines on the west and east sides of the church. This part of the service was over at 12:23 and the military guards and devil-chasers retired to the east sides of the church where each devil-chaser stretched himself prone on the ground and removed his mask. Each placed a bandana handkerchief over his head to keep from taking cold. At 12:25 the governor's staff marched out of the church and to its temporary headquarters at S22. At 12:30 the altar men took the statue of the crucified Christ from the main altar and placed it on a box in front of the Christ with the red robe. The crucified Christ wore lace "drawers" or "trousers" and a pink cape trimmed in yellow.

From 12:30 to 2:30 the members of the various societies stood or sprawled about in the shade while their women brought them *tortillas* in baskets and thick, black coffee in earthen pots. At 2:30 the devil-chasers bestirred themselves and began pulling up the crosses in the cemetery and smoothing down the graves. This rubbing out of the cemetery is an annual custom. After the *fiesta* is over a few families of persons who have died in the last year or two will come and put back the crosses and mounds, but the most of them will not. The location and identity of the graves will be lost, and sooner or later new graves will be dug into the old. The reason for levelling the cemetery is that the area will be needed for parades and dances during the next three days.

At 3:00 P.M. the devil-chaser society marched into the church past the altar and out again. They passed through the village, stopping at houses and temporary camps, returning to the church at 3:45 with three women, very old and tottering. One was almost bent double and hobbled along with a stick. In the church the three old souls knelt for a few minutes before the altar, and then they were escorted to the newly built arbor at S19, where a ceremonial feast was to be held shortly in their honor.

Mats had been placed on the ground and on these the old women were seated flat on the ground. The old bell-ringer, who was the oldest man in the village, joined them. The arbor was some fifty yards south of the entrance to the cooking compound at S17. Between the arbor, S17, and the entrance of the cooking compound in a line facing east knelt the members of the societies. The men took their positions according to rank, beginning with the governor at the head of the line at S19. Pilate and the mounted guardsmen, dismounted now, knelt in a line on the south side of the arbor. The *maestros* and singers were seated to the east of the arbor.

The feast began with a large half-gourd of water being started along the line from the cooking enclosure. Each man pretended to drink and passed it to the next man. The three old women and the old man actually sipped the water and then handed the gourd to the singers on the east. The singers partook of the water until it was all gone. Then food began to be passed along the line, each man in the line pretending, but none actually tasting, until the earthen bowl reached the old people. They would take a bit and pass the bowl on to the singers, who finished it. Bowl after bowl came down the line, *tortillas,* beans, rice, *garbanzos,* stew of wild meat, potatoes, stewed onions, and numerous pottery jars of coffee. Each person, before actually tasting the food, made the sign of the cross over it. At 4:40 the procession reformed and marched back to the church, the old people going along. At 4:43 the various societies went out of the church and a recess was in order.

At 5:42 the devil-chaser society marched back into the church and stood along the aisles. They seemed to be waiting for someone, meanwhile engaging in a great deal of horseplay. More and more women and children kept arriving. At 5:53 the three old women, with white shawls on their heads, came through a door near the front of the church. The devil-chasers then marched out with the old women, the old man going with them. They circled the village once and then the old women stopped at S2 and sat down. The man followed the devil-chasers to S20. This was an enclosure some six feet in diameter which had been made by standing in a circle of cottonwood boughs, seven to eight feet high. The old man went into the enclosure and the devil-chasers marched back to the church at a fast step. By this time the *maestros,* singers, and about sixty women had moved out from the church to S1. The devil-chasers, led by the tall figure of Pilate, went into the church, circled in front of the altar, out again, and back to S20. Three times they did this, their pace getting faster and faster. The third time they ran. We were unable to determine how the flute-player could pipe his notes at such speed. The excitement of the spectators increased with the cadence of the flute. The whole affair was working up to an exciting climax. The third time they approached the enclosure the devil-chasers threw themselves on the ground around it, their feet pointing out. At a signal they instantly pulled down the boughs. There stood the old man without clothing except for a thin breech-cloth and a crown of mesquite thorns. His body was emaciated, thin, and wrinkled, not unlike Mahatma Ghandi, and he bore a staff. The old man, representing Christ, followed the devil-chasers back to S1. As they passed S2 the three old women with the white shawls, representing the Three Marys, fell in behind. At SI, Christ spoke with Pilate. (Here the thorns began to prick the old man and he had to readjust his crown.) In the meanwhile the devil-chasers were taunting Christ and the Marys.

The procession then moved into the church, where Christ stood before the altar. Then it came out again and started on another round of the village. A rope had been placed on Christ's neck. Three devil-chasers ran in front holding the rope. The other devil-chasers threw themselves on the ground, in a row, face downward. As Christ passed he gave each a terrific wallop across the back with his staff. After each had received his blow he ran on ahead in leap-frog fashion and threw himself down to take another. So it went around the village. The old man ran swiftly, notwithstanding the fact that he was near ninety. The various societies ran behind, horsemen and all. On the return, Christ showed either real or feigned fatigue and had to be helped along by the Three Marys as he climbed the hill to the church. At SI 6 he sat down

Plate 6

14 Deer dancer on left, three "pascolas" on right.

15. One of the numerous processions of "La Fiesta de Gloria."

16. Devil-chasers preparing to burn the effigy of Judas. Note the devil-chasers' headgear on the effigy.

17. Jose Miranda, Yaqui governor of Torin, and his family.

and held a collection plate in his lap, while some of the people contributed. We could not ascertain the purpose of the collection.

The devil-chasers, military society, and horsemen made another circuit of the village, going on a run, the flute-player giving the cadence. When they returned, the governor's staff marched into the church from S22, brought out a canopy, and got ready for a general procession. It got under way at 7:02. First went a man with a black banner. Next was Pilate on his horse with a black-masked devil-chaser beside him. They were followed by three altar-boys with red dresses on. The middle one carried a cross, the other two, candles in bamboo candlesticks. Next was the statue of the crucified Christ carried by four governors. Over this statue was a canopy supported on four bamboo poles and carried by four men. Behind was the statue of the Christ in the red robe (the rope still on his neck), carried by four men. Next came three little girls in long white dresses, with paper wreaths on their heads and green boughs in their hands. They were followed by statues of Mary, Mary Magdalene, and the other Mary, one behind the other. Each was carried by four women, each woman wearing a long veil and a red crown. Behind them came the *maestros* and singers, who in turn were followed by a crowd of women and children. The procession was flanked on either side by the military society fully armed. Outside rode the six horsemen. The devil-chasers in two lines circled the entire group between each two of the sixteen crosses, one line going in a clockwise and the other in a counter-clockwise direction. The procession stopped for a chant in front of each of the crosses. It returned to SI 6 on the side of the hill east of the church just at sunset, making a colorful pageant. Back in the church again, a chant lasted from 7:55 to 8:10, when the various societies withdrew. The image of the Virgin Mary had been placed a few feet in the rear of that of the crucified Christ, and a devil-chaser guard placed over each image.

At 8:27 the devil-chaser guards over the two statues were changed. An assistant sexton brought out a lighted candle and placed it on the ground in front of the Virgin. An oil lamp was lighted on the altar and three candles placed on either side of it. For a while the *maestros* and singers chanted before the altar and then retired to a room at the left of the altar. The church was left to the images, the devil-chaser guards, a few stragglers who came and went, and the two of us who were taking notes. The devil-chasers thought they must furnish the entertainment for the rest of us. They fidgeted, scraped their feet on the ground, shook the deer-toe belts on their hips, and carefully raked the devils off the litters of the images. One devil-chaser let the other hold his rope for a few minutes while he went to the cliff to the west to get air and cough. He came back with a great deal of determination, for he shook his rattles lustily and quickly went over his image to see if any devils had taken advantage of his absence. There was chanting in the room to the left of the altar at intermittent intervals. The moon was so bright that we needed no other light in writing our notes. The talking and laughter of the military guards and the devil-chasers off duty around the campfires to the east of the church gradually died down. At 11:10 a black-shirt devil-chaser, whose status in the society is somewhat like that of a corporal or sergeant, brought in two fresh devil-chasers to relieve the old ones. The black-shirt stood some ten feet away while the four of them went carefully over the images to see that the images were properly cleansed of devils. They had to be sure that the statues were surrendered and received without taint or evil. This check over took two minutes. At 11:15 an old man came from the room at the left of the altar and muttered two sentences to each image. He bowed forward a little, but did not remove his hat. There were three Yaqui stragglers in the church now. They conversed in low tones. One of the devil-chasers accidently struck his image with his sword. This necessitated a close examination to see if any harm had been done. By this time the chanting had ceased to the left of the altar. One of the devil-chasers made a noise caused by the emission of intestinal gas. The three visitors laughed. One of them retorted with a double noise. There was laughter from the camp fires to the east. Some one out there answered in kind. The devil-chaser signaled back with two long and two shorts. The other devil-chaser guard answered with a long and a short. It began to dawn on us that they could control their noises. Then there was a whole chorus, - here, there, longs, shorts, and variations. This sort of amusement lasted twenty minutes and then died down. We did not know whether this was due to the actors' losing interest or their ability. Then things got very quiet except for the antics of the devil-chaser guards. Snores came from the room to the left of the altar. One of us went to the door and peered in. Men and women were sprawled on the dirt floor in all directions and positions. Occasionally a dog barked or a coyote yelped in the distance. At 12:08 the guards were changed again. One of the new ones was a natural clown. After a few moments he discovered the two of us who were taking notes. Then he started a show which lasted an hour. He made a stick-horse of his long sword, fought duels with a host of imaginary devils, did a variety of dances. He was especially good at a dance somewhat like a schottische. We were sorry to see him go off duty at 1:15. Nothing new happened during the rest of the night. The guards were changed every hour or two.

By sunrise on Friday morning women were sweeping the church floor and the yard and carrying water from the waterholes in the river to sprinkle the ground. They carried the water in five-gallon petroleum cans balanced on their heads. They filled the cans within an inch of the top, and with straight backs and easy steps they went up the hill to the church without spilling a drop.

From 7:00 until 10:00 several men and women were busy rearranging the altars. A large black cross was placed on the main altar. In the meanwhile the guards were taken away from the two images. Christ was supposed to be dead now. At 10:10 three women came in and started a chant. Soon the church was filling with women and children. At 10:15 the devil-chaser society began to get ready for another day of marching. At 10:20 they stomped into the church beating their swords together while their flute-player fluted. The horsemen, eight of them this morning, took their positions at the foot of the hill. At 10:32 the governor's staff arrived just behind the military society. The *maestros* had come out and chants lasted until 11:45. During this time the entire crowd went to the altar two by two, knelt, and crossed themselves before the black cross. Then one *maestro,* a very old Yaqui, came out with vestments on. These consisted of a white gown with a black cap and mantle. He lifted the black cross from the altar, and the old bell-ringer took his place beside him with a smoking incense-burner. A procession was formed which moved to the south end of the churchyard and back. The women placed their *rebozas* on the ground in front of the *maestro* in vestments and the old bell-ringer so that they did not tread upon the ground. With the cross back on the altar, a prayer lasted until 12:12. Then the various societies filed out and a recess started which lasted until 4:10 P.M.

During the recess in the early afternoon all the crosses around the village, except the large one in front of the church, had been taken out, laid flat on the ground, and covered with green branches. Over four of the crosses, at S3, S5, S7, and S10, bowers of cottonwood and mesquite branches had been erected to represent empty tombs.

At that time the boards with clappers on them were brought out, and the devil-chasers repeated the relay of the day before around the village. The various societies marched into the church at 4:50. The devil-chasers and military guards immediately came out and circled the village accompanied by the horsemen. When they returned a general procession got under way. In front was Pilate on his horse. Next came the altar-boys carrying a cross and candles. They were followed by three *maestros* in vestments, one carrying an incense-burner. Next was a bier, a frame covered with mosquito bars and paper flowers, borne by four men. These men were dressed in white sheets, and hoods on which were red crosses. Next, one behind the other, were images of the three Marys. The military guards and horsemen were on each side, and a multitude of women and children brought up the rear. The devil-chasers, as usual, continually circled the entire group in both directions. The procession stopped at the bower at S3. The bier was placed under the bower. A *maestro* swung the incense-burner in front of it, and another read a prayer. The bier was taken out and the party proceeded on around the village, holding like ceremonies at S5, S7, and S10. When the procession returned to the church at 6:20, the bier was placed before the altar, and the congregation went up in pairs, knelt before it, and crossed themselves.

At 7:20 another procession started around the village. It was like the one just before sundown the previous evening except that the two images of Christ were not there. They had got Christ buried during the afternoon, so he could not be in this procession. The governor carried the large black cross, and beside him was the army captain wearing a bonnet of feathers. By 8:00

they had returned to the church and started a chant. At 8:05 the devil-chasers retired to the east side of the church and started practicing a five-step dance. At 8:15 the governor's staff retired, but the singers chanted on until 9:00. At 9:50 some devil-chasers ran around the church three times with the clapper boards. Ten minutes later all the societies returned and organized a double procession. Pilate, the governor carrying the black cross, the altar-boys, the *maestros,* the singers, the governor's staff, half of the devil-chasers, and half of the military guards went along the usual route by S1, S2, S3, et cetera. The other group, consisting of four women carrying the image of Mary, all the other women, and the other half of the devil-chasers and military guards went in the opposite direction by S16, S15, S14, S13, S12, *et cetera*. The two groups met at S7. The governors held the cross in front of the bower. Two *maestros* knelt before the cross swinging an incense-burner. There was a prayer and chant. The other group came up and stopped some fifteen feet away. Two women crawled on their knees to the cross and waved an incense-lantern. The two *maestros* crawled to the Virgin and did the same. The processions then consolidated and returned to the church by way of stations 8, 9, 10, *et cetera*. Chants by the *maestros* and singers lasted until the next procession at 11:35 P.M. During this time Pilate sat with downcast head in a chair before the altar. The drummer of the devil-chasers sat on one side of him and the flute-player on the other. There were fifty-six women sitting flat on the ground.

At 11:28 the board-rattles were carried clapping around the church again three times. Four minutes later the governor's staff came back into the church, followed shortly by the other societies. Two processions were formed with the same personnel as before. The one going to the right carried the image of Mary; the other carried Mary Magdalene. When the two parties met at S7 the devil-chasers of one group had a sham battle with those of the other group. Then each procession continued on the way it was going to the church, arriving at 12:02 A. M. Chants lasted until 12:20, when the societies took a recess.

They returned at 12:50, and continued chanting intermittently until 1:48. Another recess lasted twelve minutes, when a procession started in two groups as before, only both parties were single file. They consolidated at S7, and marched around the village for more than an hour. At 3:20 they went back to the church for another chant. At 3:25 the societies marched out to their respective campfires. The devil-chasers were feeling unusually festive. They acted as if they were gloriously drunk. Their musicians played catchy tunes and individuals danced around the camp-fire. In the meanwhile a curtain had been drawn across the church in front of the altar, and men and women were rearranging the altarpieces behind it. The rattle-board was carried noisily around the church at 4:05. The informal dancing stopped. At 5:00 people began curling up around the fires for an hour's sleep. By 5:30 A. M. all was quiet, but not for long.

It was Saturday morning, and the devil-chasers were soon astir. It was apparent that they had some special business on hand. At 8:40 they started a burlesque parade. They had made a huge straw man to represent Judas. The figure was some six feet tall and highly sexed. This effigy with a devil-chaser's sword by its side was placed on a donkey. Behind it rode a devil-chaser to hold it on. Along with the procession went four musicians, two drummers, a violinist and one with a guitar, and twelve other devil-chasers. One of them carried an incense-burner (a bundle of rags). They did everything backwards. They went around the village in the wrong direction and approached the crosses from the back sides. When they returned they planted the straw man a short distance from the big cross in front of the church.

By 10:00 women and children were coming from all directions in holiday dress. Until this morning they had worn everyday clothing, plain, faded blue or grey calico. Today skirts were bright blue or red and shirt-waists were red, pink, green, purple, or yellow. Most of the women brought quantities of flower-petals which they placed on a pile in front of the curtain. Three *pascolas* and the deer-dancer, all naked to the waist, stood waiting at the left. People were still coming. An air of cheerfulness and holiday gayety mingled with an atmosphere of solemnity. Suspense was growing. The crowd was now far larger than at any time since the fiesta started. At 10:34 the devil-chasers stomped in, beating their swords rhythmically. All the other societies, including the *matachines,* or plumed-dancers, marched in. This was the first time either the *matachines* or the *pascolas* had appeared. The devil-chasers started a one-one glide dance step, back and forth, a line on either side of the church. The cadence gradually increased. At 10:40 the dance changed to a five-beat step, the tempo gradually getting faster. We noticed that each woman and child had filled a handkerchief with confetti and yellow flower-petals from the pile near the curtains. Dark eyes were flashing. At 10:50 the dance became a three-step. Now it was fast and furious.

Suddenly, dramatically, a bell rang and the curtain before the altar was drawn aside. The devil-chasers rushed into the inner sanctuary, while the crowd on either side pelted them with confetti, flower-petals, and green leaves. The deer-dancer broke into an orgy of dancing. In the rear of the church the *matachines* were doing a fast step. The devil-chasers stayed at the altar but an instant, when they came back, the curtain was drawn to, and they started a fast one-step. The whole episode was picturesque and seemed to represent the festive portion of the ceremonies. In five minutes the whole episode was repeated, but faster.

When they came out the second time and started a third episode, a woman, perhaps wife, sister, or other relative, took her place beside each devil-chaser and ran back and forth with him as he danced. Without losing a step each man took off a sandal and handed it to the woman, then the other sandal, next his deer-hoof belt, his anklets, and his swords. The grand climax came when the bell rang for the third time. By this time the entire crowd was worked up into a state of wild ecstasy. When the devil-chasers made the last rush to the altar the women went with them. There seemed to be some special blessing for those who got there first. They fell on their knees and the woman of each devil-chaser removed his mask and overcoat blanket, and placed a piece of cloth on his head.

While this was going on the *matachines,* plumed-dancers, became the chief attraction in the center of the church, doing a beautiful dance filled with glides, spins and turns, to the music of a violin and guitar. Each woman began leading her devil-chaser away from the altar, carrying all his paraphernalia while he wabbled as he walked. They went out to the straw man in front of the church, stuck their swords in it, and hung their masks on the swords Then they set fire to the effigy and stood by while their ceremonial property burned. One of them refused a hundred pesos for the mask he burned. He said it was a death penalty to sell a mask or a sword. The devil-chaser's part in the *Fiesta de Gloria* was over.

The governor's staff retired at 11:30. Three men with feather headdresses and bows and arrows appeared before the altar. The dancers of the military society, the coyote band, consecrated themselves for an all-night dance. The *matachines,* or plume-dancers, brought in a bamboo pole with long streamers attached to the top of it after the fashion of a May-pole. They removed their tall *coronas* and began a dance in and out, winding the streamers around the pole. The dance was beautifully and skillfully done. When wound, the streamers made a perfect design on the pole. The dancers paused an instant while their chief inspected the design on the pole to see if any error had been made. Then the dance resumed to unwind the pole. This was done without an error.

In the meanwhile the large statue of Mary had been removed from its places on a side altar and a small Mary in a little box shrine brought out. This image was dressed for the *fiesta* in a white dress, silver and gold lace, a flowered apron, a silver crown; and the interior of the shrine was decorated with paper flowers.

The military society held an altar ceremony. The men advanced two at a time holding the butts of the rifles forward. They knelt, crossed themselves and backed away. The *matachines* danced intermittently until 12:43. Several counts showed the tempo of their steps to be 108 per minute. This ended the ceremonies at the church until late afternoon. The women went to their cooking shelter to prepare *tortillas,* beans, and coffee for their families, and the men adjourned to the porch of the priest's house which was some fifty yards north of the church.

Here the *pascolas* and the deer-dancer had retired to start a dance which would last the better part of eighteen hours. There were three *pascolas* and one deer-dancer. The deer-dancer took turns with the others, but did a different dance, yet to the same music. The three *pascolas* were dressed alike, naked to the waist, a blanket around the hips, supported by a belt with bells on it, legs and feet bare except for cocoon rattles around the ankles, hair tied in a hank on top of the head like a round whisk-broom on end, a tambourine-like rattle in each hand and a black wooden mask which hung over his face as he danced and to the side or back of the head when he was not dancing. The deer-dancer was dressed in like fashion except that instead of the mask, he had a white turban-like cloth on his head. When he danced he wore a small fawn-head which was kept in place by a string going underneath his chin. [3] Three sets of musical instruments furnished music for the four dancers. One was composed of a violin and a harp, both homemade. A second was a drum and a bamboo flute, both played by an old man. A third consisted of three music sticks and a gourd-and-water drum played by four young men. The different accompanists took time about, as did the dancers. The *pascolas* did a sort of combination jig, clog, and crow-hop dance. The deer-dancer did an interpretative dance showing the movements and habits of the deer. He was a splendid dancer. The *pascolas* danced on an average of five minutes each at a time. The younger ones averaged about 340 steps a minute. The old man, over sixty, went so fast that his steps could not be counted. The musicians had near at hand earthen bowls filled with cheap cigarettes which they handed out to the spectators during the brief intermissions. They had been purchased and charged to the general *fiesta* expense account. The dancers stopped a short while at 3:00 P. M. to eat.

At 6:25 all the societies including the dancers began to assemble at the church for a procession. The devil-chasers were without their masks and other paraphernalia. They were now a tired, bedraggled, serious group. One would not suspect them of being the restless, clowning demon-rustlers of yesterday.

The procession moved directly from the church to S21 where a new arbor, some twenty by twenty feet, had been constructed in the course of the day. About every fifty feet along the way the group stopped, and all those in front of the canopy turned and faced it for an instant. When the image of Mary had been placed under the arbor, the *matachines,* candle-boys, altar-boys and girls dressed in white danced back to the church and disbanded at 7:25. Apparently the arbor, S21, was to be the center of the night's ceremonies.

About 5:00 in the afternoon the gaunt old ox which had been tied to a palm tree in the plaza for two days was killed. Eighteen dogs attended the slaughter, but little did they get, as the Yaquis utilize practically every bit of a slaughtered animal. Now the meat, including the intestines, was being roasted in the cooking compound at S17.

Piles of dead, solid mesquite wood had been stacked near the new arbor earlier in the day to furnish fires for the night. Shortly after sundown a number of fires were lighted, the military society having by far the largest one.

The *maestros* and singers chanted in front of the arbor until a church bell rang at 8:00. At 8:10 there were fireworks. At the same time the *pascolas* and deer-dancer started a dance under the arbor. They rotated continuously until

44

9:25, when they rested for a while. About this time the *matachines* started a dance in the dimly lighted church, a dance much like our Virginia reel. They had no audience; everyone was at the arbor, S21, but they went on for an hour without stopping. They did not dance again until next morning.

At 10:20 the coyote dance started a short distance west of the arbor. It was a monotonous dance done by three warriors wearing feather headdresses. Each straddled a long bow, stick-horse fashion, and beat a cadence on the bow with a split piece of bamboo. The three went abreast keeping the left foot about six inches in front of the right, doing little crowhops. They went back and forth, beating out trails some thirty feet long in the dust. The coyote is the most uninteresting of all the Yaqui dances.

The *pascola* and deer-dances went on under the arbor and the coyote dance in front of it periodically all night. The *maestros* and singers chanted occasionally. Only the devil-chasers and children slept. The devil-chasers had their own camp-fire around which they sprawled, using rocks, chunks of mesquite wood or nothing for pillows. They had earned their rest, and slept like logs. The women in the cooking compound kept a tub of coffee and two tubs of stew boiling. Some of them were busy cooking tortillas. From time to time food and coffee were carried out and served to the people. The night was crisp and still. A round moon shone above the palm trees in the old plaza. Nature had conspired with the dancers to create an atmosphere of mysticism. So great was the effect that we hardened materialists who were taking notes felt it and were moved. We experienced to a small degree the fascination these occasions have for centuries held for the Yaquis.

Before daylight a cold wind sprang up from the Northeast. People huddled closer to the fires. Even the dogs with their hides drawn tightly over their ribs edged in. There was a lot of coughing, deep down in chests, caused by four nights of exposure on the cold ground. A woman and two children slept shiveringly under a thin blanket with a dog on the foot of the blanket. Dawn began to appear. The military society formed a double line facing the East with hats on the ground at their feet. It was an early morning silent prayer. This officially ended the coyote dance.

At 6:00 there were fireworks. Ten minutes later the military society, with their guns this time, and the governor's staff, formed in lines and marched to the church, bowing to the cross in front as they entered the church. The governor and chiefs of the military society went up to the altar, knelt and crossed themselves and returned to their places. Candles were lighted on the altar. Then followed an initiation of two boys into the military society.

The warriors with all their arms were in single column on either side of the church. At either end of the space between was a *maestro*. One boy was about seven and the other about nine. Each was given a flag and a feather headdress. A member of the society in a feather headdress went about with them. An old man walked behind the three apparently to prompt them. The boys were first conducted to the altar, where they knelt and crossed themselves. A *maestro* and chorus chanted. The chorus consisted of one man and one woman. Then the boys were marched back and forth a number of times, up and down the church, while the warriors held their guns at a forty-five degree angle. Then there was a long prayer by the *maestro* at the north end of the column while the boys stood with bowed heads before him. This was repeated by the *maestro* at the south end of the column, and then the one at the north end gave a second prayer. More marching back and forth and waving of flags. The warriors formed a circle with the neophytes and a woman in the center, for more prayers and flag-waving. The ceremony lasted thirty minutes.

The *matachines* had spent the night at the church. At 7:00 they went down to the cooking compound to eat. They returned to the church at 7:25 and started one of their beautiful, whirling dances. The *pascolas* and deer dancer were still performing at the arbor. Shortly before 8:00 the devil-chasers, just ordinary looking Yaquis now, but somewhat refreshed after a night's sleep, started setting a double row of boughs some eighteen feet apart from the arbor to the church, a distance of about 500 feet. They were getting ready for the journey of the risen Lord from the tomb (arbor) to the church. The lines were laid off by a Yaqui dragging his sandled feet through the dust. The green cottonwood boughs, twelve to eighteen inches high, were placed about every three feet. At 8:25 the bell at the church was rung to announce that the *avenida* was complete.

Drum-beats at 8:55 announced that the triumphant procession was about to get under way this Easter Morning. Fireworks. At 9:02 the church-bells rang, and five girls with the image of Mary ran from the church down the avenue of green boughs. About halfway they turned and ran back to the church. At 9:06 they ran out again, got nearer to the arbor, but turned back. At 9:11 they came out again, almost reached the arbor, turned, and ran as though the prairie were afire behind them. At 9:15 seven of the *matachines* quietly left the church carrying their *coronas,* plumes, and rattles in their hands and went to the arbor. Three minutes later the other seven *matachines* started dancing in the church. At 9:21 a procession formed at the church. The seven *matachines* led, and they were followed by three *pascolas.* Behind them came three girls dressed in white, with flags, followed by twelve women bearing images of the Three Marys. Four other women held a canopy over Mary, the Mother. More than a hundred women and girls followed behind. They were going to meet the risen Lord who was approaching from the East.

The procession of Jesus had formed at the arbor. In front were three coyote dancers, dancing backwards, followed by seven *matachines* with their whirls and glides. Then came one *pascola* and the deer-dancer. They had scarcely stopped since noon the day before. Next were the altar-boys with flags followed by four men carrying the image of Jesus under a canopy. As the two pro cessions approached they would go a short distance each and stop with a system of responses. When they met, the dancers stepped aside, and there was flag-waving and incense-burning by each group. This was solemn enough, but it lasted only a minute or two. The Marys then recognized the Christ, and what joy, — fireworks, confetti, flag-waving, and wriggling of images! The two groups then formed into one and proceeded to the church. First went the altar-boys of one group, then the coyotes, the fourteen *matachines,* the four *pascolas* and deer-dancer, the girls dressed in white, the altar-boys of the other group, the four images all abreast, the *maestros,* singers, and multitude. As they slowly went up the hill to the church the bells chimed, and the dancers danced furiously. The military society flanked the procession on both sides. The devil-chasers without their paraphernalia were solemn and subdued. When the procession reached the church, Jesus was mounted high on the main altar, and Mary was placed on the ground at his feet. The other Marys were placed on a side altar at the left. Everyone knelt except the military society. The devil-chasers removed their sandals and placed handkerchiefs over their heads. There was a chant by the women singers. Four days and nights of singing in the open air was causing old High Pitch to get hoarse.

While the chant was going on we counted 218 persons present. A baby was crying lustily. She was trying to tell the congregation that she was getting tired of these endless processions. The mother finally compromised and offered the child a huge, full breast. The baby disgustedly rejected it. We had an idea that she had the stomach-ache. The mother carried her out, and we could hear High Pitch again.

At 10:10 while the chant was still going on, the *matachines* started a slow dance in and out among the kneeling worshipers. Chants, prayers, and dances lasted until 11:30, when a final procession was organized. It was in the same order as the previous one, except that there were but two images, a small one of a seated Jesus, and the Mary in the little box shrine. The two were carried side by side under a blue canopy. We thought they were going around the town as usual, but they fooled us and went around the church instead. It was soon over, and the congregation listened to a final chant by High Pitch. The *pascolas* and deer-dancer left at 11:50. We imagined they were glad to get away, as they had been at it for twenty-four hours. There was a general hand-shaking in front of the church. Part of the people lined up in a "receiving line" and the rest circled around and shook hands with them several times. At 11:58 it was all over but the drinking. The habitual drinkers had abstained from their mescal for forty-five days, and it had been going hard with them. Before sunset there were more than a dozen lying here and there in the streets of Torin with froth in their mouths, a red, glazed look in their eyes and streaks of mud made by the mixing of dust and sweat over their bodies and in their hair. So ended the *Fiesta de Gloria.*

[1] Erna Fergusson in article, "Yaqui Pascola" published in *Mexican Life,* April 1935, describes a Fiesta de Gloria which she witnessed at Tlaxcala. The ceremony was performed by a group of Yaquis who had been forcefully moved to the

State of Morelos by Porfirio Diaz. The Tlaxcala fiesta contains all the essential parts found in the Torin ceremony. The sequence of events are not quite the same; for instance, the devil-chasers, or Fariseos, burned their masks and wooden swords at Torin on Saturday morning, while at Tlaxcala the burning took place on Sunday morning.

[2] For description of cocoon anklets see Frances Densmore's "Yuman and Yaqui Music", *Bureau of American Ethnology Bulletin,* 110, pp. 155-156. The cocoon has been identified as "Rothschildia jorulla." A similar cocoon has been reported from Abilene, Texas, by Dr. Cyrus N. Ray.

[3] For a description of the deer-dance as given by Arizona Yaqins see Frances Densmore's "Yuman and Yaqui Music," *Bureau of American Ethnology Bulletin,* 110, pp. 155-165. Miss Densmore also gives a detailed account of Yaqui musical instruments.

Chapter Four - Yaqui Funerals

William Curry Holden

Yaquis love funerals. They live in a state of constant expectancy from one funeral to the next. One can never tell for certain when the next funeral will be, and this very uncertainty holds a charm. Who knows but before the day is over the bell at the Yaqui church will toll, announcing to the Yaqui world that the time has again come for an all-night *fiesta,* and, perhaps, if the deceased is venerable enough, for a celebration lasting for two days and nights or more.

Our first experience with a Yaqui funeral occurred at Torin in March, 1934. One Saturday evening, when we had just eaten our supper, and Ramon, our interpreter, was making a pair of sandals for our physical anthropologist, one of the three bells on the Yaqui church began to toll. Ramon, wise in such matters, announced that some one was dead — perhaps old Anita; for days her death had been expected, if not to say awaited.

At eight-thirty a solitary candle was lighted on the altar at the church. About nine-thirty three of us started out to find the funeral. We were still leery about going into the Yaqui section after dark. The soldiers at the Mexican garrison had told us how treacherous the Yaquis were, and how easy it was to get a knife-blade between one's ribs. We knew the Mexicans might be stringing us along as tenderfeet, but we noticed that they stayed as far from the Yaquis as they could after sundown. So we approached the Yaqui garrison with considerable caution. We had though it best to go there first and get permission from the chiefs to attend the funeral. The second army chief was the only one at the garrison, but he seemed pleased that we were interested and offered to take us himself. He led us first to a cross on the east side of the hill on which the church is located. Here the devil-chaser society was assembling. As we arrived they were putting on their masks and forming in two lines. Presently they marched to the church, making a rhythmic beat with their wooden swords. They circled inside the church, got an old kerosene

Plate 7
18. Funeral procession leaving church.
19. Corpse in cemetery where it has just been measured for the grave dimensions. Man on extreme right is laying off the grave.
20. Open grave after corpse has been deposited. Note bones on the pile of earth at right.
21. Typical graves in cemetery at Torin.

lantern, and came out. As they left the church they were flanked on each side by a line of Yaqui warriors fully armed with cartridge belts, high-powered rifles, automatic pistols (with hammers cocked), and knives stuck in their belts behind. To the tune of a bamboo flute and drum the entire party marched to the house where the dead woman lay. We followed.

The area inside the compound was lighted by a number of camp fires. Under an open lean-to shed at the east end of the house was old Anita, for it was she, on a straw mat with a candle burning on either side of her. At her head was an improvised altar made of a covered table bearing an image. Several women sat flat on the ground nearby.

In the yard, about thirty feet south of the corpse, planted in the ground was a small cross, some four feet high. A small area of earth, three or four feet in diameter, had been dug up just south of the cross. In this loose earth were stuck the staffs of the four chiefs, the banners of the eight clans, the spears and swords of the mounted guard society, and the wooden swords of the devil-chasers. On each devil-chaser's sword was his mask.

Two of the mounted guards took two spears and stuck them in the ground at Anita's feet, crossing them, making an "X." Then men and women started coming singly or in pairs, kneeling before the spears at Anita's feet and crossing themselves.

Meanwhile more people were arriving and the yard was filling. Presently, the chiefs decided that more room was needed, for this was to be an extraordinary funeral. A group of men proceeded to move the fence on the south side, cutting the horizontal bamboo pieces with their big knives, pulling the parts up and carrying the fence away in sections. In three minutes it was done.　Two or three men were keeping the fires going. Under an arbor a short distance east of the corpse, several women were sitting flat on the ground, cooking *tortillas*. Near by a tub full of coffee was boiling. Lots of it would be needed to keep the crowd awake for two nights. And the dogs were there, — perhaps a hundred all together, slinking about, snarling and fighting. Each woman cooking *tortillas* had a stick with which she whaled every dog within reach.

There seemed to be no definite ritual scheduled for the night. The crowd was just milling around and kicking dogs out of the way. We stayed an hour. Having been informed by Ramon that nothing else would happen that night, we went back to camp and to bed. After we were in bed, we could hear a native musician playing a mournful dirge on a bamboo flute. He would start on a high note, hold it for some time, and then slur off on three lower notes. The flute was going every time any of us was awake during the night. Occasionally, we heard chanting. Beginning about daylight, homemade fire-crackers, somewhat like our sky-rockets, were shot, a feature which Ramon explained by saying that when a soul started up to the gods these rockets helped to boost it along; that each rocket hiked it up a little farther.

About sunrise, as we watched through field-glasses, some thirty men went down the river and came back with poles, cottonwood boughs, and bundles of bamboo cane. No ceremonies occurred in the course of the day. Ramon had promised to come for us as soon as the night affair got under way, but at nine o'clock there was no Ramon; so we decided we were missing something and started without him. At the funeral compound we found Ramon, and learned his reason for not coming for us: his chief had told him to cut wood, and the power of a society chief being next to absolute, Ramon was cutting wood.

Everything was in full swing, illuminated by firelight and candles. A new death arbor some eighteen feet square and built of the cottonwood and bamboo which we had seen the men carrying, had been built in the open space south of where Anita had lain in state the night before. Three sides of the arbor were open, but the west side was closed with cottonwood boughs. In the northwest corner was an altar, on which stood two images. Near the front of the arbor, suspended by a thong from the ceiling, was a bucket of water with a gourd in it. Some thirty feet east of the arbor was an open-air altar, on which were a cross and twenty-five or thirty small hand-made books that looked, from where we were, like packages of fire-crackers. Ramón said they were books containing the names of "all the dead peoples".

Just west of this altar was Anita on a brand-new bier. Her bamboo litter had been elevated eighteen inches on four poles with forked ends. Anita had been re-dressed since the night before. Now she had on a blue dress of cheap cotton cloth. On her body tied to her waist, was a stalk of cotton, evidently grown the year before, with open bolls. Plain brown stockings, the only stockings we saw on a Yaqui, covered her feet. A black cap was on her head, and her strong old wrinkled face was uncovered. Her hands were tied together across her chest with a blue string. Her head rested on a small blue pillow. Everyone seemed quite concerned about the comfort of Anita's head. Every little while someone would come around, lift her head, and rearrange the pillow. We could not see that they were helping matters any, but they evidently thought they were. Around the bier on tall, bamboo candlesticks were eight candles which clearly illuminated the body.

A few feet east of the open-air altar was a cross planted in the ground, and behind it, after the manner of the night before, were chiefs' staffs, and the arms, banners and masks of the various societies. A dozen fires scattered about the place not only gave light but helped to ward off the chill of the night.

On each side of the corpse was a devil-chaser in full attire, — mask, overcoat blanket, deer hoof belt, and anklets of cocoon rattles. In his right hand each had a long, painted sword. In his left he had a short wooden sword and a green mesquite branch, — the symbol of immortality. These fellows clowned, did antics, made countless passes with their wooden swords at imaginary devils over the body of Anita. About every forty minutes the devil-chaser chief "changed guards". The change was accompanied by a special clownish ceremony. The new and old guards would jump around, make a series of passes at each other and end the ceremony by backing up to each other with a severe butt. The devil-chasers' vigil over the corpse went on all night. Regardless of what else took place they anticked and kept the evil spirits shooed away.

From nine to ten o'clock the ceremonies were predominantly pagan. Under the death arbor a couple of deer-dancers took turns at dancing somewhat like a combination of our tap and buck-and-wing dances. Their costumes consisted of a short blanket around their middles; bell-adorned belts around their waists; and cocoon anklets on their legs. Both were barefooted. When they danced they wore a black wooden mask made grotesque with long horsehair whiskers. When not dancing, they hung the mask on the side or the back of their heads. Their hair was bound in a hank so that it stood up straight on their heads like a round whiskbroom. A part of the time they danced to the tune of two home-made violins played by two stolid Yaquis at the rear of the arbor. The rest of the time the music was of a more primitive type. An old man sat on the ground and played a flute and a drum. An official fire-tender kept a bed of live coals near the drum so that its heads would stay tight. Two younger Yaquis played music-sticks. It was the business of the two dancers to entertain the crowd. While they were not dancing they made jokes, — as Ramon put it, "they make funny words". Their jokes were in Yaqui, but the Yaquis have incorporated a number of Spanish words, so that we could get the drift of what they were saying. They took several cracks at us. One was on *el patron,* another was about *los Americanos* who could not say anything but *si, señor* and *muchas gracias*. The crowd laughed heartily. We had the feeling, however, that the dancers were better at dancing than at wise-cracking. One of them, an old man over sixty, was good.

While the dancing was going on, the women were systematically feeding the crowd. A half dozen women were cooking *tortillas* made of wheat flour. The dough, made in large batches, was somewhat like our lightbread dough. A woman would take up a ball and start patting and revolving it on her forearm until it was eighteen to twenty-four inches in diameter and as thin as a piece of cloth. Then she would throw it into a large, flat earthen bowl over a hot bed of coals. Almost as soon as the *tortilla* touched the bowl, she would turn it over with her fingers. In a couple of seconds she would fold it over double, then flip it over, then unfold and refold the other way, then over again. Then she pitched it to a woman on one side who put it in a basket. When finished, the *tortillas* had the consistency of pie crust. With a half dozen women cooking, the woman who put them in the basket was kept busy. The coffee tub was kept boiling at one side.

End to end, on the ground, were bamboo mats, on which the women placed a basket of *tortillas,* a bowl containing a few lumps of sugar, (the only sugar we saw them use) , and a couple of coffee pots. Fifteen or twenty men would stack their hats by the cross east of the open air altar and silently file around the mats, kneel down, and pass the basket of *tortillas* around. Coffee was served in pottery bowls, each holding about a pint, and two, three or four persons used the same bowl. They never used over one lump of sugar to a bowl of coffee. Behind those eating stood a dozen or more men and women, each holding a burning candle. The effect of the whole scene, the men kneeling reverently around the mats, eating *tortillas* and drinking coffee, the candle bearers standing behind, silent and rigid, all reminded one vividly of a communion service. When one group finished eating they left and others came. Usually the men ate first and then the women, but there seemed to be no fixed rule, for at times men and women ate together.

At ten o'clock the nature of the ceremony changed. Two young women representing the two societies to which women belong, came and knelt at the foot of the corpse, one on either side. Each woman wore a black *mantilla* over her head upon which was a red crown, and in her hand was the red banner of her society. This each continuously waved, energetically and deftly, cutting various and complicated figures in the air with it.

Eight mourners came and knelt on narrow mats some distance farther back from the foot of the corpse. Behind the mourners was the priest society, consisting of the native priest (*maestro*), two assistants, and a dozen women. On either side of the corpse knelt the plumed-dancers, their brightly-colored headgears and the brilliant plumes which each held in his left hand giving a festive appearance to the scene. The headgears matched the paper flowers on old Anita's dress. Just outside the row of plumed-dancers, standing in double columns on either side of the corpse, were members of the military society, fully armed.

A flute with its four-note dirge was played periodically, accompanied by a drum. The priest society chanted. The native priest, dressed in the usual denim and sandals, would chant a line and the women would chime in a few measures behind. The women were led by a fat woman, weighing over two hundred and fifty pounds, with a shrill soprano voice. The most of her two hundred and fifty pounds was around her middle, and when she sang, it heaved up and down like a bellows. We called her Old High Pitch. When she sang, one could not hear any of the other chanters. Her voice carried more than a half mile.

Chants were interspersed with prayers led by the priest. He said them in a continuous rolling monotone. After more than an hour of chants, prayers, and flute and drum dirges, this formation broke up.

Then for a while the performance which had taken place from nine to ten was repeated, — the deer-dancers doing their buck-and-wing steps, and "making funny words," the devil-chasers still driving the devils away from the corpse, men and women partaking of food again. The women cooking tortillas had never stopped. Occasionally there would be fire-works, and Anita's soul would be propelled a little higher.

So it went all night, pagan and Christian observances mingling. Babies cried and sometimes choked. Several of them had whooping-cough, *hooptia*, the Yaquis call it. Dogs barked, snarled and fought. As the night wore on, children went to sleep. Their mothers bedded them down at the edge of the crowd under thin blankets. The night was chilly. We buttoned our sheepskin coats around our necks and edged up to a fire occasionally. We wondered how the children clad in thin calico could stand it on the cold ground. They sleep like logs, however, unless overtaken by a coughing fit. By midnight the women were all looking tired and worn out. This was the second night of it. Some of them curled up near the fires for a nap, but not for long. There was still more cooking to be done, and more chants to be chanted, and more dogs to be driven away from the *tortilla* basket.

One of our party stayed to see the ceremony through the night. The rest of us went to camp and to bed, but not to sleep as soundly as we wished. Periodically through the latter part of the night the flute's dirge or Old High Pitch's voice awoke us, and we would lie awhile and look at the rounded moon going down in the west and wonder about funerals.

The next morning about nine o'clock as we were passing the Yaqui garrison on our way to see how the funeral was progressing, we noticed the four chiefs and the entire military clan gathered there. We stopped in to shake hands with all of them. It is a breach of etiquette to pass a Yaqui without shaking hands the first time you meet him in the day. That is, if he is a friendly Yaqui; if he is not friendly, one had better not meet him. Before we got through handshaking we heard the funeral procession coming up the road from the east, and we moved quickly so as to see it.

In front came the fourteen plumed-dancers doing a beautiful dance full of movement, glides, turns, spins, — all in unison. Red, yellow, blue and purple streamers fluttered from the tops of their tall *coronas*. Brilliant plumes of parrots' feathers, red, yellow, white, and green, waved in their left hands, and gourd rattles beat a fast cadence in their right hands. The three youngest members, boys about eight, ten, and twelve, respectively, wore long white, stiftly starched dresses. One wore a red slip under his dress, one an orange slip, and one a green slip. The other eleven wore brilliantly colored scarfs around their shoulders. All of them wore the native sandals.

Behind the plumed-dancers came the devil-chasers in full array, masks and all, jumping, clowning, wielding their wooden swords, and making terrific passes at imaginary devils along the way.

Next came four men and four women carrying on their shoulders the bamboo litter with Anita's corpse on it. Forty hours had passed since she died, but her wrinkled old body was so thin and emaciated and the air was so dry that decomposition had not yet begun. The litter-bearers walked in a sprightly manner, jiggling the body up and down to the cadence of the plumed-dancers' steps.

Next came the *pascolas* with their wooden masks hanging on one side of their heads and the muscles in their naked bodies looking surprisingly fresh after twelve hours of dancing. Then came the *maestro* and his assistants and old High Pitch and her assistants. Behind them were the drummer and the flute-player still piping his four mournful notes. A multitude of women and children followed.

The procession stopped in front of the Yaqui garrison and the pallbearers lowered and raised the corpse five times in front of the cross there. The four chiefs and members of the military society marched out from the garrison in two columns, flanking the procession on either side. The entire group then moved towards the Yaqui church (a combination of pagan shrine and Christian church made of bamboo) on a hill a quarter of a mile away. They paused for a moment before a cross at the foot of the hill to lower and raise the corpse five times more and then proceeded up the hill to the big cross in front of the church.

They placed the body on the ground at the foot of the cross and spent twenty minutes in chants and prayers. In the meanwhile one of the assistant chiefs measured the length and breadth of Anita's body with a couple of bamboo sticks. He cut them just the right length. The corpse was then carried into the church and laid on the ground before the altar in the north end. The priest and the chorus started a chant which lasted an hour.

In the meanwhile the assistant priest had measured off a grave in the south end of the church. A devil-chaser, who had removed his mask, brought a spade and started digging the grave. He kept his measuring sticks close at hand so as to take no chances on getting the grave too large. None of the other Yaquis took any interest in the grave-digging. After a while a second devil-chaser came and relieved the first one, who went away and did not come back. The only ones taking any interest in the digging were members of our expedition. The devil-chaser dug into another burial. , He threw out a thigh, a leg bone, an arm bone, a few ribs, and a number of finger bones. That made no difference; he paid no attention to them.

When the grave was finished to a depth of three and a half feet, and a couple of bamboo sticks crossed over it, two girls dressed somewhat like Greek Catholic bishops came and waved red banners over it. They were consecrating the grave and driving the evil spirits out. Next the devil-chasers in masks came in two lines and circled the grave three times, one line going in a clockwise direction and the other line going counter-clockwise. Each devil-chaser cut vigorously in the air with his wooden sword.

The procession then formed and brought the body to the grave. The litter was placed on the pile of dirt by the side of the grave and Anita's hands were untied. Several men lifted the body from the litter and handed it to two men in the grave. The litter was thrown over the cliff at the edge of the church yard. The two men lowered the body into the grave. They seemed to be in a great hurry. Anita's head got turned to one side and her mouth fell open. The only pains they took for her comfort was to place the little blue pillow under her head. They did not straighten her head or shut her mouth. We watched carefully to see if they would pull a cloth over her face, but they did not. The men got out, and the priest standing at the head of the grave sprinkled in some water and some earth, mumbling a few words.

The procession retired to the church and started another chant. Three or four men and a half-dozen women stayed to fill the grave. A man pitched a spade full of dirt into Anita's face. Some of it went in her mouth. One man spaded and the women pushed the dirt in with their hands. When the grave had been filled about a foot with loose dirt, another man brought a tamper. It consisted of a square granite rock weighing about twenty-five pounds with a wooden handle mortised into it. The man got down in the grave and began tamping. His first move was to whang right down over Anita's face. More dirt and more tamping and they got the old lady firmly tamped in. The bones which had been thrown out were pitched back in as if they had been clods of earth. They had little excess dirt left over, and this was made into a small mound. A little bamboo cross was placed at the head. All this time skyrockets were being fired nearby.

When the grave was filled, the priest society came and knelt around the grave, and the head priest said a prayer. They returned to the altar in the church and started another chant. The devil-chasers came and circled the grave three times in the same manner as they had done around the open grave. When they went away, the relatives came and knelt about the grave. This was the first time they had been near the body or the grave. They had come to the church and remained apart from the crowd until now. The oldest one among them, an old man, said a prayer. Then they arose and went to the large cross south of the church where they arranged themselves after the fashion of a receiving line. Friends of the relatives formed another line and started around shaking hands with them. A Yaqui handshake is a ceremony in itself. Each person touches his own left shoulder, then the other person's left shoulder, and grasps the other's hand on a backward movement. There is something collegiate about it when done rapidly. Each friend circled around and shook hands with each relative three times.

The military clan formed into a column of threes and marched back to the Yaqui garrison. Not a tear had been shed, but Anita had been highly honored. Very few Yaquis rate a forty-two hour funeral. The most of them are lucky if they get more than a twenty-four hour ceremony.

We thought the funeral was over, but we found out three days later that we were mistaken. Another all-night session would be necessary to commit Anita's soul safely to its eternal home. It seems that the Yaquis are a trifle confused as to how and when a spirit leaves a dead body. If the person is unmarried they assume that the ascension is immediate. When the person is married they are not so sure whether it is at once or whether the soul stays three days in the grave and then comes out to start its heavenly flight. Anyway, they take no chances on it and hold a second all-night ceremony on the third night after the burial of every married person.

It was nine o'clock when we went down to the ceremonial grounds, the same place where the funeral had been held. The people were forming a procession at the edge of the clearing a hundred yards east of the death-arbor. The order of the procession was similar to that of the funeral except that the pallbearers carried a litter on which was an image of the Virgin. The group moved slowly to the death-arbor, where, in the main, the schedule of the second night of Anita's funeral was repeated. Chants and prayers alternated with *pascola* dancing and feasting throughout the night, with an occasional shooting of fire-works. At sunrise the ceremony ended, and the people went home. We were told that one year from that night a similar affair would be held for Anita.

The people got one night's sleep before starting another funeral. About four o'clock the next morning a man about thirty-five died, presumably of tuberculosis. A few hours later a little girl, a beautiful child of two, died of whooping-cough. The bodies were dressed for burial and carried on bamboo litters to the place of death ceremony. They were placed on a crude table under the south side of the arbor. The man was dressed in a robe of black calico. There was nothing on his head, and his feet were bare save for a pair of new sandals. These had been cut from the hide of a black cow. The hair was still on the soles of the sandals. Flowers cut from colored paper were attached to the man's shoulders, elbows, wrists, chest, knees, and ankles. By his side was a devil-chasers' sword. The child was dressed in pale blue calico with numerous paper flowers attached.

A crowd of people and dogs milled around the place all day, but the ceremony did not start until about dark that night. The procedure was the same as in the case of Anita's funeral with one exception. Seven arches of bamboo cane had been erected in a line in the course of the day. The arches were about thirty feet apart, and each was about eight feet high and eight feet wide at the base. About nine o'clock a procession formed with the same general order as in Anita's second ceremony. Instead of the images, they carried the two bodies side by side. The procession moved under the arches to the easternmost one and then returned.

The march to the church got under way early the next morning, for the man was stinking. The child was buried first, while the man's body lay on his bamboo litter before the altar in the church. It seems that only one spade was available, so the measurements for the man's grave were not taken until after the child was disposed of. When the man's grave was finished they rushed him into it with great speed. No effort was made to get him in a comfortable position. His eyes were half open and his jaw had fallen, but the men who placed him in the grave were anxious to get him covered up, for the stench was sickening.

About ten o'clock of the first night of the *Fiesta de Gloria,* a baby seven months old died of pneumonia. We speculated as to whether the Yaquis would take time out to hold an all-night wake while the *Fiesta* was on. About eight the next morning while we were eating breakfast we saw half a dozen women coming up the hill towards the church. One woman had something on her head. When the group came nearer we saw it was the corpse of the baby on a little bamboo litter. The mother and father, whose ages were eighteen and twenty, preceded the little procession to the church. The parents went into the church, where they stayed until the burial was over.

The woman placed the corpse on the ground at the foot of the large cross. A man came and measured the body for the grave dimensions. It was a mite of a grave not over two feet long and a foot wide. About thirty inches deep, the man came to another body. Instead of digging a new grave, he levelled the bottom so as to put the baby squarely on top of the skeleton beneath. While the grave was being dug the body remained at the foot of the cross. Four or five women sat flat on the ground near it, talking and laughing.

When the grave was finished we thought the devil-chasers would surely come and march around it. They were nearby, as the *Fiesta* was in progress, but took no notice of the burial. When the women started to the grave with the corpse a flag-waver ran to the grave and waved his flag over it briefly and hurried back to the shade of a tree where he sprawled on the ground. As the body was placed in the grave the *maestro* and three or four women came from the church where they were busy with *fiesta* proceedings. The priest sprinkled water and earth in the grave, said a short prayer, and returned to the church. Four women and the man who had dug the grave filled it, the women using their hands and the man the spade. He tamped the dirt in as had been done in the three previous burials. When a little bamboo cross had been planted and four candles lighted over the grave, the parents came from the church and knelt with four other persons whom we took to be relatives. As several prayers were said, the mother, a comely woman, wept, the only weeping we saw at any funeral. After a few moments the relatives went and stood before the cross in front of the church. Friends came and went through the customary handshaking.

A fifth funeral was in progress the day we left Torin. As we bumped along the dusty road we heard skyrockets exploding above the sands of the Yaqui river, each one sending the old man's spirit a little higher up to the gods.

Chapter Five - Household Economy

William Curry Holden

An inventory was taken of the utensils of fourteen kitchens. Every kitchen had a large *metate* of porous volcanic rock for corn grinding. Only one *metate* had the short triple legs so common in Mexico (Figure 5, Plate 2.). Six of the remaining thirteen were mounted about thirty inches high on mesquite posts. The women using these stood as they ground their corn. The other seven *metates* were mounted on blocks of wood or rocks a few inches above the ground. The women used them in a kneeling position, which would soon become back-breaking for a white woman. The Yaqui women have two ways of grinding corn on these *metates,* the wet method and dry method. The wet method is used more frequently than the dry. About a gallon of corn is soaked overnight in water and wood ashes. As the woman grinds it with a *mano,* it becomes a soft pasty dough which is caught in a wooden bowl placed under the lower end of the *metate*. It requires an hour or more to grind a gallon of corn. A little salt is added to the dough, and the woman pats it into a *tortilla* which she cooks on a large, flat earthen bowl over an open fire-place. When the dry method is used the corn is placed in a large olla over the open fire place. A woman constantly stirs the corn with a long wooden spoon. Many of the grains will crack open slightly as does popcorn. The rest becomes brown and crisp without cracking. The woman then grinds the corn on the *metate,* after which she mixes it into dough by adding salt and water. *Tortillas* prepared in this way have altogether a different texture and flavor from those made by the wet method. The average woman puts in from three to six hours a day preparing corn-meal and cooking *tortillas.*

Seven of the fourteen kitchens had mechanical corn-grinders. All of these have been purchased during the last few years since the government began paying the Yaquis "to be good." These grinders, which sell at ten *pesos* each, resemble our hand sausage grinders or food choppers. A woman can grind her corn in one of them in a fourth of the time required on a *metate.*

Eight of the fourteen kitchens had separate *metates,* of smaller size, for coffee grinding. Three kitchens had small mechanical coffee-grinders, the kind which is nailed on the wall or a post and which is used by frontier people in this country. The Yaquis trade for a native, green coffee of small size. This the women parch in large *ollas* in a manner similar to parching corn, only it takes much longer. When made into coffee it is as black as tar and has the consistency of thin soup. It has a vile smell and a viler taste. Yaquis drink it black, occasionally using sugar. Thirteen kitchens had coffeepots made of cheap porcelain or tin. Eight of these had two pots each and two kitchens had three pots. These are new innovations taken up since the government began paying the Yaquis. Formerly they used earthen *ollas* of their own make for coffee pots. In one kitchen an *olla* is still used.

Each of the fourteen kitchens contained from one to six five-gallon square tin cans, the kind used by oil companies the world over. The Yaquis cut the tops out of them and insert a handle by nailing a rounded piece of timber across the center of the can just below the rim at the top. The cans are used principally for water carrying. Most of the water is carried by the women. A woman can balance a five-gallon pail of water on her head and, if need be, walk for miles without spilling a drop. On an average, the homes are located about a quarter of a mile from the river from which most of the families get their water. A few use wells. Several families visited by our party lived from two to three miles from the river, and all the water used was carried from it either on the heads of the women or the shoulders of the men. Men never carry water on their heads; instead they carry two five-gallon pails at a time, each suspended from the ends of a stick across the shoulders. (Figure 27, Plate 11).

Each kitchen had from two to five tin or zinc buckets varying in size from a half-gallon to two gallons. Nine kitchens had a steel or cast-iron skillet each, and one kitchen had two. The other four used pottery vessels instead of skillets. All the kitchens had from one to ten earthen cooking-pots. Beans, next to *tortillas* the chief item of food, are always cooked in *ollas,* which vary in size from one to two gallons. A pot of beans is cooked and then kept simmering constantly for two or three days until eaten. Then another potful is cooked. (Note bean pot in Figure 35, Plate 12).

Eight of the fourteen kitchens had from one to five tin or porcelain cooking-pans of some sort. The other six had no kind of metallic cooking-pans whatever. Five kitchens had cheap porcelain dishpans. The other nine used wooden or pottery bowls for dishpans. Practically every kitchen has one or two wooden bowls. (Figure 19, Plate 3). These vary from fifteen to twenty-four inches in diameter and from four to seven inches in depth according to size. Somewhere in nearly every kitchen will be hanging from one to five canteens. These have been stolen or captured from the Mexican army from time to time.

Thirteen of the fourteen kitchens had from two to nine porcelain cups each. No china cups or plates were seen anywhere. Five kitchens had forks, from one to five each, and four had knives, from two to five each. The only knives seen in the others were long homemade hunting-knives similar to the ones the men wear behind their belts. The average Yaqui has little use for table-knives and forks. He eats most of his food with his hands. He takes a *tortilla* from a basket, cups it in his hand, puts in a spoon full of beans from the bean pot, folds the *tortilla* together, and eats it as a sandwich. It is only when there is a stew of *javelina* or deer meat, which is not often, that he needs an eating implement, and then he generally uses a spoon. Only one kitchen of the fourteen had no spoons. The others had from two to ten each. The spoons were cheap and much like the ones that sell two for a nickel in our five and ten-cent stores. Twelve of the fourteen kitchens had from one to six porcelain plates each. Thirteen kitchens had smoothing irons, two having one and eleven having two each. These irons were heated on mesquite coals. They were much thinner than traditional irons used in this country.

Every kitchen we visited had from one to ten baskets each. There was always a *tortilla* basket from ten to fourteen inches in diameter and six to eight inches deep. Then there was usually a larger basket in which the eating utensils were kept. This basket, when the utensils were not in use, was kept near the hearth, or hanging on a wire attached to a log in the roof. There might be other baskets, of varying sizes and shapes, for storage purposes. Eight of the fourteen kitchens had a homemade table each. These were usually very crude and wobbly.

The different kitchens had various miscellaneous objects. Number 2 had a piece of sheet iron over the open fireplace instead of the earthen griddle on which *tortillas* are cooked. Number 3 had a saddle, an American steel-trap, a leather pouch, and three sleeping-mats. These stood against the wall during the day and were spread on the floor at night. Yaquis sleep on them without removing their clothes and with only a blanket for cover even on the coldest nights. Number 4 had two little, old trunks, probably captured in a raid on some Mexican ranch, a rifle, a rawhide rope, two cow-hides, several mescal bottles, and a leather pouch. Number 5 had a brush broom and a small porcelain sugar bowl. Number 6 contained three homemade chairs. Number 7 had one chair and two rawhide stools. Number 8 had a crude cupboard in one corner. Number 10 had a swinging pot-rack, twenty by fifty inches, hanging from the roof. Number 11 had a baby cradle. Number 12 contained an improvised cupboard made of two pine boxes.

We took inventory of the bedrooms of the fourteen house-groups containing the fourteen kitchens mentioned above. In all we minutely examined twenty bedrooms, as there are sometimes two bedrooms attached to each kitchen. The contents of bedrooms are not so uniform as are those of kitchens. They are used not only for sleeping, but for storage of practically everything the family has which is not found in the kitchens. In fact the bedrooms are a combination of sleeping quarters, clothes closets, harness and saddle rooms, tool sheds, attics and cellars — all in one.

Rather than attempt to generalize about their contents, as in the case of the kitchens, it will be easier just to pick out a typical bedroom and give its contents in detail. In room A of house-group 5, for instance, was an elevated bed on the east side. It was mounted on two trestles made like our carpenter's "saw-horses," only not so high. These were about fourteen inches in height. Across the horses were small round poles about one inch in diameter and six feet, six inches long. They were close together. On them was a bamboo sleeping-mat. Piled in a heap on the back side of the mat were a faded blanket and two crude pillows, stuffed with raw wool. This type of bed is not common, as perhaps nine-tenths of the Yaquis sleep on mats thrown directly on the ground. Hanging on the wall behind the bed were several items of clothing and a pair of sandals. Against the north wall were leaning two sleeping mats. Above them attached to the wall was an old tin bucket filled with odds and ends. On the west wall were hanging two saddle-bags, a dancer's rattle, plumes, and headgear, a small mirror, a bag woven from the *carrizo* tops filled with knickknacks, a water-canteen, a rifle and cartridge-belt, a monkey-wrench, and an old colored shirt. On the south wall were a few lengths of chain, a horsehair rope, a rawhide lariat, and several small crosses made of *carrizo* blades. In the southeast corner were two five-gallon tin cans on which was placed a pine box filled with a jumble of women's clothing. In the southwest corner were standing several agricultural implements, two weeders, a long-handled spade, and a wooden spade used for winnowing grain. In the northwest corner were a saddle, a set of dilapidated harness, and some bridles. On a pine box near the center of the room was a large *carrizo* basket containing about a bushel of beans. Hanging from a roof-support above the bean-basket was a sack containing about a peck of shelled corn. The room had a generally untidy appearance.

Somewhere in practically every Yaqui house, either in the kitchen, a bedroom, or under a shed connecting the kitchen and bedrooms is a large earthern water *olla* mounted on a three-pronged post (Plate 9). The *olla* usually has a capacity of ten to fifteen gallons. It is porous enough to permit the water to seep through and collect like "sweat" on the outside. Sometimes there is a slow drip from the bottom of the *olla.* The drip is drained off by means of a little trough and caught in a pottery bowl buried even with the surface of the ground. This becomes a drinking-place for the chickens. In time a green mass covers the outside of the olla. The water on the inside is extremely cool even on the hottest days. It seems to be a matter of custom with the Yaqui women to keep the water olla approximately full all the time. We were told that they occasionally scrub out the inside of the *olla* in order to keep the pores open so the water will continue to "sweat" through and make the olla cool. The dipper usually consists of a half-gourd.

Practically all of the household work is done by the women, washing, ironing, corn-grinding, cooking, water-carrying, sewing, which is done mostly with their fingers, sweeping, and wood-carrying. Wood-carrying requires considerable time. As a rule Yaquis burn only dead solid mesquite. As the supply becomes exhausted near the camp the women have to go farther and farther from their houses for it. It is not unusual for a woman to walk a mile or more, break up a bundle of wood, tie it with a leather thong, (Figure 7 Plate 3), balance the load on her head, and carry it home. All of this she usually does while her husband sits at the council-house and spits.

We were astonished one day when we entered the house of one of the most prosperous families and found a Singer sewing-machine. It was an old-fashioned pedal model which was made perhaps twenty-five years ago. We were unable to learn how the family had come into possession of it, but we suspected it had been captured in a raid. The full-breasted, smooth-faced woman who used it did sewing for other people. She charged fifty *centavos* for making a skirt or shirtwaist. She said she was busy all the time with outside sewing.

During the month of March when the nights are chilly, the sun feels warm and inviting until the middle of the morning, although it gets hot enough during midday. Frequently we saw Yaqui women sitting flat on the ground in the sunshine, as is their custom, combing one another's hair with a burr from the organ cactus. These burrs are about the size of a turkey's egg and are covered with sharp spines. They ripen in the spring, and the women gather numbers of them for use throughout the year. The women burn off some of the spines on two sides so that the burr can be grasped by the thumb and fingers. The rest of the spines are trimmed to a uniform length. The burr then serves effectively as both a comb and brush.

The woman's hair is long, straight, and black. If time permitted after the combing, the women would delouse one another. One woman would take little "lands" about a half-inch wide on the other's scalp and go up and down snapping the lice between her thumb nails (Figure 22, Plate 11).

In their dress the men wear any kind of shirt they can get, blue denim trousers, and straw hats of many varieties. The women wear several calico skirts which are gathered at the waist with draw-strings and a short loose shirt-waist which is not gathered at the bottom. In public they wear brown or black mantillas over their heads. At home, they frequently wear bandana handkerchiefs. All the men and part of the women wear sandals; the rest of the women go barefooted. Very little jewelry is worn by men or women; such as was seen is like that sold in our ten-cent stores.

Chapter Six - Yaqui Architecture

William Garrett McMillan

Yaqui architecture is based on the use of wood and bamboo (*carrizo*), being influenced by building materials immediately at hand. In structural design the supporting framework consists of "Y"-shaped vertical supports set in the ground, and horizontal logs of varying sizes and crookedness placed overhead (Plate 9). On this framework are placed purlins of small size, spaced at intervals of twelve to thirty-six inches. The framework is then ready for the walls and roof of bamboo, which grows in abundance along the Yaqui River.

For the supporting columns and horizontal beams, mesquite logs are commonly used, although in some instances cottonwood and willow are preferred. The low ceiling height of the houses is influenced by the fact that the forked mesquite trees do not offer very long vertical posts without involving excess diameter and crookedness. The normal roof height is about six and one-half feet at the eaves. The necessary hip or pitch in the roof at the center of the houses is usually obtained by placing a short auxiliary log immediately under the beam at the crotch of the vertical support.

In placing the roof on the log framework, a heavy layer of unstripped bamboo poles is placed at right angles to the purlins of various sizes and uneven lengths. The process is again repeated with the several layers of bamboo at right angles to the previous layer (Plate 9). The number of layers depends upon the spacing of the purlins and the subsequent thickness of the water-repellant dirt placed over the roof area. Growing vegetation during the rainy season is sometimes in evidence on the roofs. In some cases where there is no apparent need for protection from seasonal rains, the roofs of unstripped

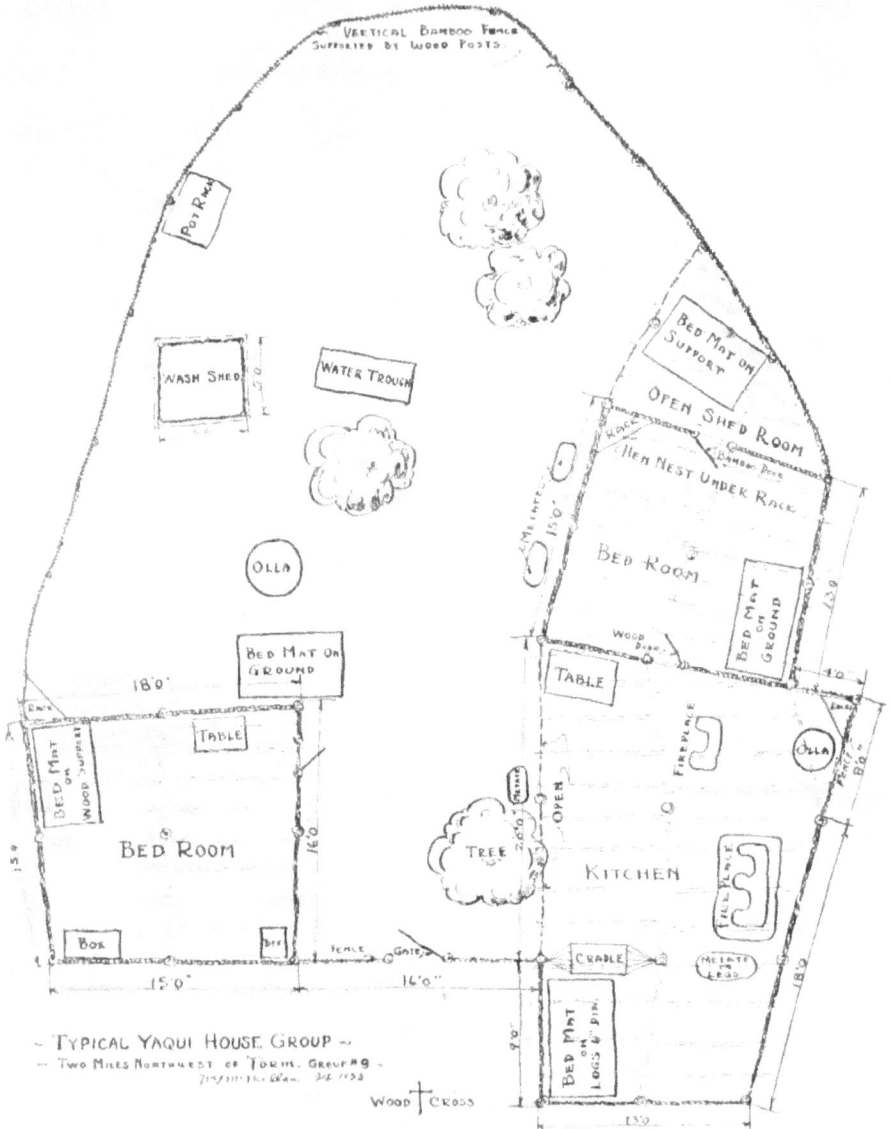

Plate 8 - Plot of a typical Yaqui house group.

BLANKET LINED POLE CRADLE.

CORRAL GATE

ADOBE 3" TO 5" THICK

ALTERNATE LAYERS OF BAMBOO

HORIZ. WOOD BEAMS

PURLIN - WOOD BLOCK

VERTICAL BAMBOO

BARE TIES

'Y' COL. SUPPORTS

HORIZONTAL BAMBOO

COLUMNS SET IN DIRT

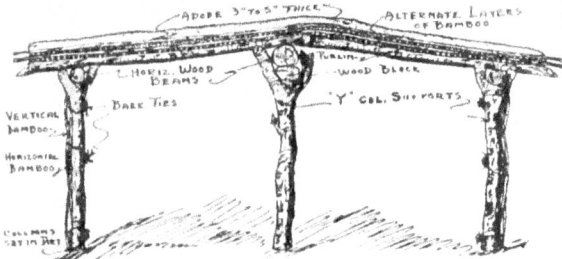

TYPICAL SECTION THRU HIP TYPE CONSTRUCTION.

HAND HEWN MORTISED CHAIR

WATER WELL, WOODEN CHUTE & LIVESTOCK WATER TROUGH.

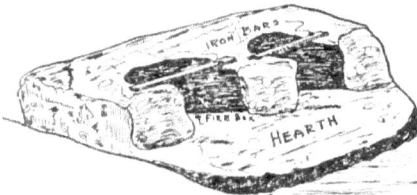

IRON BARS

FIRE B.

HEARTH

ADOBE & STONE KITCHEN FIREPLACE.

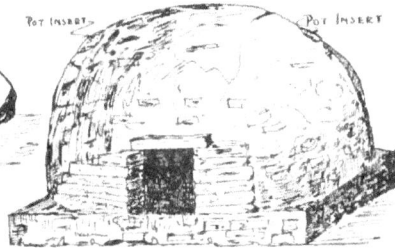

POT INSERT

POT INSERT

POTTERY BURNING OVEN

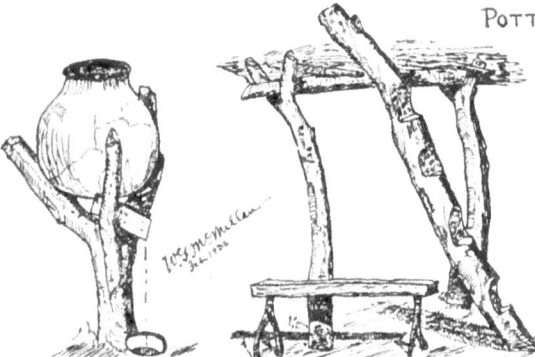

LOG DOOR SILL.

OLLA OR WATER VESSEL.   BENCH, LADDER & 'Y' ROOF SUPPORT.   LOG CHICKEN TROUGH

Plate 9 - Yaqui architectural details.

65

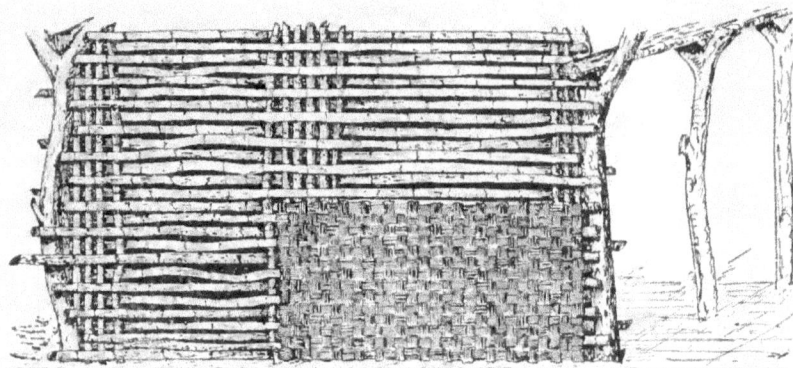

TYPE 'A' HORIZONTAL WEAVE (ONE IN-ONE OUT) AND FLAT WEAVE.

PLAN OF HORIZONTAL WEAVE.

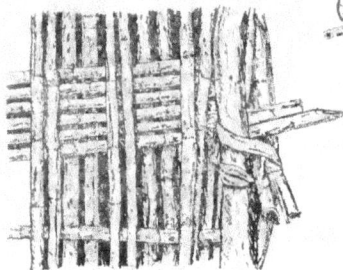

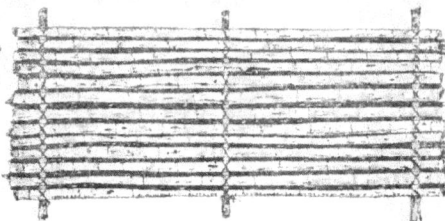

BARK TIE AT CORNER POST.   DIA. BARK TIES ON DEATH MAT.

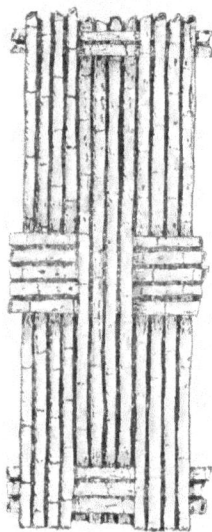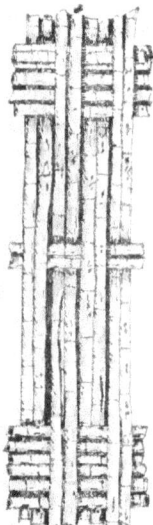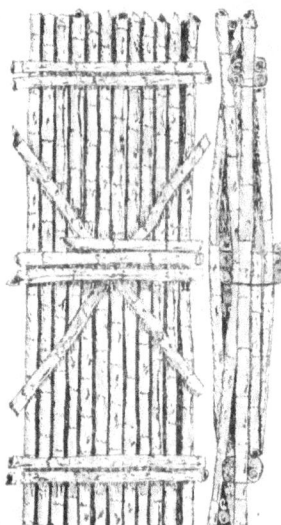

TYPE B·4   SECTION   TYPE 'B·2'   SECTION   DIA.& HOR. BRACING   SECTION

TYPE B VERTICAL WEAVE.

Plate 10 - Yaqui wall types.

bamboo are held down by means of larger bamboo poles bent to the contour of the roof and securely tied to the supporting beams and purlins with bark ties. Where a shade from the heat is desired, the roof is often-times a series of wood poles close together, tied down with bark or wire. The hip type of roof predominates in the larger houses. Smaller rooms are sometimes built adjoining the larger structures and are covered with the lean-to or shed type of roof.

The walls are built by interlacing the bamboo poles at right angles to one another. The prevailing types of wall and fence construction are the horizontal and vertical weaves with the vertical weave in its various forms predominating (Plate 10). The walls are occasionally plastered with adobe. The horizontal weave (A1, Plate 10) is best suited for the reception of the adobe plaster mud. This weave, however, requires longer lengths of bamboo to reach from column to column. There is no fixed number of vertical interstices in this weave, but in nearly every case observed the central part of the span contained from six to twenty verticals. At the ends and near the supporting columns there are several verticals to hold in place the horizontal members which may not be long enough to reach the columns. Types "A-1" to "A-3" (Plate 10) weaves are used.

In making the vertical type of weave, two or more long bamboo poles are lashed by means of bark, rags, or wire, usually bark, to the bottom, center, and top of the supporting columns. As the work of lacing the vertical members progresses, the horizontal members are added in varying numbers at the center and top sections. The most commonly used types of vertical weaves are "B2" and "B-4" (Plate 10) although "B-1" to "B-6" types are in evidence. There is no preference shown in regard to the supporting columns projecting on the inside of the walls. In some cases where the flat bamboo mats have served their usefulness as beds, the mats are tied in place with bark strips to the exterior walls (Plate 10). Sometimes when the old walls need repairing, another wall of the reverse type is applied over it (Plate 10). This wall is given additional security by placing diagonal and horizontal members to the outside surface.

There is no treatment for the dirt floors other than an occasional sprinkling of water administered at the time of sweeping. The black soil reaches a powder fineness when dry. Where the floors are moistened regularly and subjected to daily sweeping a hardness comparable to adobe is obtained.

The only window in all the houses visited by our party was a small opening in which there were bars consisting of vertical sticks spaced about three inches apart and mortised top and bottom to the log frame. This window had the appearance of an observation point. Windows are not needed in Yaqui houses. The cracks in the bamboo walls permit sufficient ventilation and a ready escape of smoke from the kitchens.

The doors are of several types. The accordion type, with the bamboo or willow members laced in a vertical position by means of three horizontal rawhide or bark thongs, is fastened stationary on one side and is allowed to fold back when loosened on the opposite side. Another type involves three horizontal wood members to which the vertical members are laced or nailed at about three inches spacing. The outer vertical members of the hinged side rest on a pivot at the top and bottom and are encompassed by a forked limb which, in turn, is nailed to the supporting door post. In isolated cases milled lumber, nails and hinges are used. Large logs are staked down for door sills to prevent the ever present dogs from digging under the doors and gaining admission to the houses (Plate 9).

Gate construction is identical with that of doors except in the case of corral gates. These gates consist of heavy, movable individual poles which slide in slotted inserts at the heavier gate posts (Plate 9). Wire ties are used to reen-force the retaining posts.

Fence construction is represented by three types of material. In the residence fence enclosures the vertical type bamboo weave is used almost exclusively. In some instances, instead of bamboo, smooth or barb wire is used as the three horizontal interstices. The mesquite supporting posts are placed at irregular intervals and with no apparent regard for straight lines (Plate 8). Often a growing tree large enough to serve as a post is a decided influence in the shape, direction and size of a fence enclosure. Only in isolated cases is there any attempt made to cut the vertical members a uniform length. All the vertical types of weave are represented in the fence enclosures. Where strength is needed for retaining livestock, heavy wood construction fences are used. The more open type of fence is executed by means of vertical posts set in pairs at varying intervals with horizontal logs securely cradled at the supports. Another less popular type is a solid fence erected by placing vertical posts close together and setting in the ground. These solid fences are about six feet high. Barb wire fences are in evidence around the more prosperous households. Natural fences in the form of cactus growths are pruned from the ever present and abundant thorny vegetation.

The composite house groups are influenced by the size of the families (Plate 8). There is no attempt made for a systematic arrangement or for symmetry in the enclosures. The bedroom with the four walls is adjacent to the open sided kitchen, which usually has a higher ceiling than the other roofed structures. The open kitchen permits unhampered escape of smoke and easy access for hungry dogs, chickens and birds. Often a kitchen is large enough to accommodate a bed mat or baby cradle. There are never more than two rooms in an individual unit. As the growing family needs more space, separate bedrooms are constructed nearby, the main kitchen serving the requirements of the entire group. A fence enclosure affords more privacy and security from the ravages of prowling dogs and vermin. The enclosure may encompass small storage sheds, pens and chicken houses, pot-racks, sunshades, farm and ranch implements, garden plantings, and the like. Many groups are scattered over wide areas with no organized setup or privacy.

Generations of life close to nature have taught the Yaqui to utilize her products for his daily needs. Ladders, work trestles, chickens and stock water-troughs, shovels, boats and many other necessary commodities are carved from the soft grained woods growing in abundance along the river banks (Plate 9).

Chapter Seven - Medical Practices of the Yaquis

Charles John Wagner

The Yaquis are a fairly healthy people. Evidently some immunity is created against bacteria to which a race is constantly exposed. Travelers in Sonora are usually promptly afflicted with dysentery to which the Yaquis are not subject, but tuberculosis, rare among them, is rapidly fatal once it is acquired. Immunization against disease is practically unknown to them. Even small-pox vaccination is rarely used. Isolation to prevent the spread of disease is also little known. On a Saturday night during the pre-Easter festival, when many had assembled at their brush-arbor temple, thirty-eight children were counted under four years of age — many were babes in arms. Among the thirty-eight, eighteen had whooping-cough.

The first sick call, after the Yaquis satisfied themselves that our party included a physician, was to a shelter among the ruins of the former Mexican city of Torin, We found a young man dying of tuberculosis. He lay on the usual bamboo mat on the earth floor of the common living room. Dust on the floor was shoesole deep. Food was being prepared at the fireplace in one corner. Utensils were used in common. Three children were playing about the room, A babe sat on the mat near the sick man's head. As he coughed he expectorated first to one side then the other as the presence of playing children permitted. The physician's inability to do much for the sick was offset in this case by the great opportunity to help the living.

Diseases prevalent are whooping-cough, pneumonia, diptheria, malaria and typhoid. Epidemics of small-pox occur and are wide spread. Venereal diseases, so common among the neighboring Mexicans, are not common among the Yaquis as these people do not intermingle. Tuberculosis was encountered at Torin where Yaquis were living in adobe ruins where sun and the air had not free access as in their usual bamboo shelters. One case of pellagra was seen — several of rheumatism. Malnutrition was rare. Skin diseases are apparently infrequent. Some throat troubles and middle ear disease were found. Their teeth, in spite of the lack of care, are fairly sound. Tumors are numerous and neglected as scarcely any surgery is practiced.

Ordinary treatment is generally known among the Yaquis as household remedies are known among us. Headache is treated with curative moistened leaves held to the head by a folded moistened cloth. Fever is controlled by teas and by moist cloths or leaves applied to face and wrists. Cathartics —

Plate 11
22. Women catching lice in each other's hair.
23. Women water carriers.
24. A potter at Torin.
25. Wash day at a water hole on the Yaqui River.
26. Another wash scene.
27. Our interpreter, Ramon Torry, carrying water.

herbs eaten or taken as tea — are used, while dysentery is controlled by other herbs. Small wounds, abrasions and ulcers are covered with curative wood-scrapings or leaves, and bandaged. The Yaquis understand something of the value of rest and limitation of diet. There are few cripples among them, attesting to the fact that those critically injured usually die.

Yaqui medical practices contain little of magic, but some superstitions persist. When a child is born it is a common practice to wind a strand of tendon fiber loosely but securely about its wrist. As long as it remains, the child will not have whooping-cough! Among us the asafetida bag is still worn about the neck and the potato carried for rheumatism, but we hide them in our clothing.

Childbirth among the Yaquis is not often accompanied with trouble. The mother is usually attended by older women in the family or by some experienced woman as a midwife. Two case-histories were obtained where mothers were unattended, managing the event themselves, even to the tying of the cord and the disposition of the afterbirth. Severe distochias usually result in the mother's death. The medicine man is rarely called. After delivery some mothers are up at once, but the usual custom is for them to stay on the bed mat from three to five days.

Children are welcomed and much loved, but the death rate among them is appalling. It is not unusual for a woman to have borne eight to ten children with only two or three living. The mortality is not at childbirth but within the first six or eight years when whooping-cough, diphtheria and small-pox take their terrible toll.

The water-supply changes with the season. When it is dry and the river is very low, drinking water is obtained by digging pits in the sand and dipping the water that rises. During high water when the river is muddy, villagers use a common well near the river. Outlying settlements are supplied with water carried from the river, as their wells are usually brackish. The supply of water for drinking and cooking is kept in an olla supported on a tripod in the shade of the house. Sufficient water filters through so that it is kept somewhat cool by evaporation. The drip is caught in a bowl on the ground, thus affording a drinking place for the chickens and dogs. Dogs usually outnumber the people of a household. They are useful as settlement scavengers — rarely fed, but otherwise well treated. Washing of clothing is done at the river or in water-filled holes near the shelter. Their infrequent bathing is also done at the river.

They sleep in their clothing with one blanket on a mat of interlacing flat bamboo laid on the bare earth. When not in use during the day these mats are leaned against a support in the sun to be thoroughly dried and aired. These Indians have very few possessions. Almost any Yaqui can pack what he cares to take and be on the move in five minutes. With these facts in mind a better understanding of their health and medical practices is possible.

The Yaquis guard the identity of their medicine men as well as the medicine men's remedies with great caution. Time and again, while at Torin in the course of the first expedition, we undertook to meet the medicine man, but our interpreter and guides did not know where he was, or he had gone away, or he was too busy to see any one, *et cetera*. Later we learned that we had passed his house several times each day. On the second day after we arrived at Torin, on the second expedition, we had a long conference with the chiefs. After the governor had made a long and warm speech of welcome and had offered to co-operate with us in every way they could, we asked anew to see their medicine man. The chiefs conferred at length. Finally the governor said that the next afternoon he, himself, would take us to see their native doctor.

The next afternoon the governor kept this appointment. The medicine man was near fifty, an earnest, dependable man. He brought out his medicine pack with as much frankness as his people had previously shown reticence concerning him. His medicines were contained in a cloth some three feet square. The opposite corners were tied together as one ties a small pack in a handkerchief. He spread the medicines out on a crude table, and for three hours carefully explained to us the uses of each.

For dysentery the medicine man takes three small sticks of *goma de Sonora* and boils them in water. Then he adds *cominos* (anis seed), cinnamon bark, and essence of mint. This mixture is strained and some alcohol added to preserve it. The patient is given the equivalent of a small whiskey glass three times a day.

Diarrhea is treated with *molanisco*. The root is beaten to a pulp. This is steeped in cold water, and the liquid is taken several times a day.

There are three remedies for headache. One is of *bailburia* root, dried, beaten to a powder, and mixed with tallow forming a salve. This is applied to the head. A second remedy is made from mesquite leaves. A quantity of these are mashed into a pulp. This is mixed with water and urine, made into a poultice and applied to the forehead. The third remedy is made from the bark of *cuhuca* (*huisache*). A strip about one inch in width and two inches long is beaten to a pulp. This is moistened with urine from a male and applied to the forehead. The poultice is allowed to stay on until the odor becomes so offensive the patient cannot stand it any longer.

For typhoid fever a preparation made from the immortal plant is used. The leaves and fine stems are boiled and made into a tea. This is drunk at intervals. It is very bitter and probably contains quinine.

For scarlet fever the yellow root of the *mochi* plant is used. It is beaten to a pulp and steeped in cold water. The liquid is placed where the dew will form oh it overnight. Beginning next day it is given to the patient three times a day for three days. During the time the patient eats no food.

When a patient is delirious he is given a warm tea made from the leaves and stems of the *lia* plant. He drinks a cupful every half-hour.

Earache is treated with a preparation made from beef gall. It is dried in its own sack in the sun. Several thin slices are steeped in water. About half of a teaspoonful of the liquid is dropped in the patient's ear. The same medicine is also used for toothache.

For hiccough a tea made from the seed of the *torito* plant is used. The seeds from one pod are ground and steeped in water. The patient sips the liquid until he gets relief. The *torito* plant grows south of Sonora in Sinaloa.

There are two remedies for rattlesnake bite. One is very simple. The *golondrina* (milkweed) plant is mashed to a pulp, and the paste is applied to the bite. The second remedy is more complicated and must be made in advance and kept on hand. A snake is killed, its gall bladder taken out, and the gall mixed with an equal part of alcohol. The mixture is allowed to stand for twenty days. It is then ready to apply to the bite. The medicine man does not permit his patient to drink any water for several days, as he believes it will cause the poison to spread. The juice of the century plant is applied to sores. The plant is mashed in such a way that the juice falls directly on the sore.

For cuts and bruises a more intricate preparation is made. The *yerba del monzo* is beaten to a pulp. Rosemary, *yerba colorado,* and *alucema* seed, all beaten to a pulp, are added, making a paste. This is applied to the cut or bruise.

To prevent whooping-cough, the common practice, as mentioned above, is to place a tendon around the child's wrist. He sometimes wears this for several years. Another remedy is to wear around the neck a little bag containing nutmeg, flax seed and aniseed. This is also good for preventing other diseases. After there has been a case of whooping-cough it is customary to fumigate the house by burning Spanish dagger in it.

Small-pox is treated with a tea made from *amapa* (dye wood). The wood is scraped in water causing it to turn to a light orange color. The tea is drunk half a cupful at a time. It has a delightfully cooling taste. Another medicine for smallpox is got from a small black insect called *pinocate.* It is put into water where it gives off a yellowish excretion. The liquid is then drunk. This is done about the time the patient breaks out. In about six days the patient gets well.

For coughs, a tea is made from the bark of the *torote* tree. The tea is boiled and a half cupful taken three times a day for six or eight days.

For a blow on the chest, as when one is kicked by a horse, the resurrection plant is used. The plant is placed in water, and when it begins to grow the patient drinks the water. If the plant fails to open up, it means the person will die. Pains in the chest and back are treated with paste made of white caliche powdered and mixed with urine from a boy not over fifteen years old. The paste is applied as a poultice on the place of pain. I he caliche is obtained near Nogales, about three hundred miles to the north. The remedy is somewhat like our use of antiphlogistine.

For a blow in the stomach a medicine is made from *palo mulato* bark and *cochana* root. These are boiled together and made into a drink. Only a little is taken at a time as it is very strong.

Lung troubles are treated with a remedy made of the roots of *yerba de la vibora* (snake grass). The roots are mashed into a fine powder. This is put into water in a vessel and beaten vigorously until it froths. The froth is skimmed off and put on the chest.

Gas relief is obtained from a brew made from mesquite bark. The bark must come from the tree on the side of the rising sun. A strip of bark is beaten into a pulp and then steeped in water. The liquid is drunk as needed.

Cathartics are made from various herbs. One very commonly used is a tea made from the macerated bark of mesquite twigs.

Fainting spells are treated with a medicine made of Brazil wood and mesquite leaves. The Brazil wood is scraped into a glass of water. This colors the water a light red. The mesquite leaves are mashed and put into water. The liquid is then taken internally.

Pinkeye is treated with the juice from *haicocoa* berries. The berries are about the size of buckshot and of a deep red color. The juice is mashed out and smeared on the eyes, temples, forehead and cheeks.

Abortions are sometimes produced by drinking a tea made by boiling *corcho* (a cork-like pine) in water. A lump of sugar is put into a cupful and drunk once a day for three days. It makes the woman deathly sick. She has spasms and occasionally becomes perfectly rigid. Another kind of tea for the same purpose is made from the roots of the immortal plant.

Sometimes abortions are produced by mixing the resin of the *brea* tree with tallow and making a paste. This is rubbed on the abdomen. When this remedy is effective it is probably due to the severe rubbing instead of the paste. Another way to produce an abortion is for the woman to press her abdomen across a tree or rock.

Hemorrhoids are treated by inserting in the rectum a conch shell, heated and covered with tallow. It is inserted in a twisting manner.

Hydrocephalus (water on the brain) is treated with nutmeg. The nutmeg is ground into a powder and rubbed on the temples.

For ant bites the Yaquis use the wax from the mesquite tree. In the last few years this practice has been modified by the use of commercial glue, which is smeared over the bite.

The Yaqui remedy which interested us most is one which is purported to cure rabies. Scores of persons told us that they had seen Yaquis cure patients who had already started having spasms before the treatment had begun. Among those who claimed they had witnessed such cures were two Americans who had lived many years in Sonora and a number of Mexican army officers. There seem to be three or four remedies. The one by which most store is placed is a tea made from the bark and leaves of the *fresno* tree. This tree is said to grow in the mountains. Only *atole* is given the patient to eat. If he becomes irrational he is tied up until the medicine has its effect.

Another remedy when *fresno* tea is not available is made of beans. About a pint of beans is roasted and then ground very fine. This bean meal is mixed with cold water. The patient is made to drink the mixture until he vomits. The next day the treatment is repeated. If the patient is not better it is repeated again on the third day.

A third remedy for rabies is made from the *golondrina* (milkweed) plant. It is used in two ways. Some of the weed is mashed and made into a paste. This is applied externally over the bite. Some of the weed is mashed, steeped in water, making a tea. When it settles, the liquid is drained off and drunk. The patient must be careful not to get any of the weed as he drinks.

The governor at Torin told us that he once had seen a Yaqui cure a patient of rabies in Magdalena by the rubbing of saliva all over him. The treatment went on two or three days, during which the patient fasted. The governor mentioned also, without apparently knowing the significance of the remark, that the Yaqui who gave this treatment was known not to have been effected by the bite of a rabid animal. This "cure" can be given some credence. In the treatment of certain diseases, as diphtheria, we use the serum from the blood of animals in which immunity against that disease has been created. Serum from the blood of individuals recovering from measles, mumps and infantile paralysis is used with success in the treatment of those diseases. This leads to speculation about the possible formation, in the body, of principles antagonistic to the virus of rabies, that could be transmitted with curative effect through the body fluids as in this case, the saliva. Mother Nature has taught primitive man many things through experience that scientific men are discovering in the laboratory.

Gunshot wounds are treated in a primitive but effective way. A section of bamboo having about the diameter of the wound is selected. Another piece with closed end is fitted into this, making a crude popgun. Brazil wood scrapings are placed in this "gun" which is then inserted and wound forced full of the scrapings. These, in contact with the tissue fluids, swell, stopping hemorrhage. As the wound heals this plug is extruded. In the absence of anything better, severe wounds are plugged with a mixture of grass and moist earth. Very little is accomplished with abdominal or chest wounds, which are usually fatal. If a person so wounded can be moved, he is usually carried into the mountains.

Fractures are placed in as good position as possible by manipulations and then splinted with split bamboo.

Throughout the medicine man's explanations one could not but be impressed with the fact that these people were doing the best they could with what they had at hand.

The medicine man at Torin said that it took a lot of work to keep up his collection of herbs and medicines. They had to be collected from over a wide area. He had to go as far as three hundred miles for some of them. With the utmost frankness he said that none of his remedies were sure. He added that they were not so reliable as the white man's medicines, but they were all the

Yaqui had, and he and his people were forced to get along with them, the best they could.

On the occasion of our second visit to his shelter, after painstakingly explaining his remedies, he gave us many specimens, pieces of his valuable woods, herbs, and some appliances which he could duplicate. Interesting hours were spent several times in the mutual exchange of information. We showed him our physician's bag with its medicine kit, the surgical supplies and instruments and the diagnostic apparatus. He, and the fringe of Yaquis listening, seemed especially interested in the blood pressure apparatus. They were pleased to have it used on them. We gave the medicine man a metal box of ready dressings, a bandage scissors, a pair of dark glasses, a bottle of iodine (the color was pleasing), a tube of ointment and some simple remedies, all of which we explained. He was very appreciative and listened with careful interest as we talked about the benefit of cleanliness, safeguarding water supply, the use of antiseptics, and the purpose of isolation in contagious diseases. The Yaquis are eager to learn. On the other hand we learned much from them.

We were privileged to minister to many. Their confidence and gratitude were delightful. Nine came for operations. The first, of course, was the most eventful, as we felt that the patient had volunteered or had been selected to "try out" the surgeon and much depended on the outcome. Our group had been in the Yaqui village about ten days when Juan Serrano, who had frequented the camp, came asking us to remove a bullet from his spine. He walked with a waddle as the result of a gunshot wound across the back which he said he had received nineteen years before, in an engagement with a Mexican force. As he was crouching behind a rock, he was shot repeatedly across the back, the bullets plowing a groove just above the hips. It had been a year before he could walk again. On examination we found the condition as he stated. A large bamboo cane could easily be laid in the deep scar across his spine and on pressing deeply a hard movable particle could be felt to the right of the last vertebra. We explained to him that in our country a foreign body like a bullet in a critical location is not removed unless it is giving trouble. He answered that he wanted it out because "It makes pain in the light of the moon." So we agreed to remove it for him. He then said that it would have to wait because it would be two days before he could take off his clothing. This was true, as a *fiesta* was then in progress, lasting four days and nights, during which they did not remove their clothing. On the morning after the *fiesta* we went to the Yaqui officers' headquarters, where we had arranged to perform the operation. The crowd was there but Juan was not. We could not miss such a chance of gaining the Yaqui's goodwill, so we did the unheard of thing here — we hunted up the patient. We found Juan at his home shelter and although he looked a little surprised, he came with us willingly, bringing an earthen basin with water in which we were to scrub our hands. Our surgical bag contained two surgical packages, a large one, in case a major emer-

Plate 12
28. Deer-dancer.
29. A sick Yaqui. Note the bundle of leaves tied around his forehead.
30. "Pascolas" and musicians.
31. Reed fife and drum player.
32. Dr. Wagner and the Yaqui medicine man at Torin.
33. Coyote-dancers.
34. The expedition's water hole dug in the sand of the Yaqui River bed.
35. An elevated cooking hearth.

gency operation for one of the party was necessary in the jungle, and a smaller package of sterile supplies and instruments, such as were needed for the operation at hand. A squared log used as a bench at the edge of the headquarters' stone porch served as an operating table. Juan lay face down on the log with his arm as a pillow . His back was bared. The small package of sterile instruments was laid near him. Every member of our group assisted. Two, with tree branches, warded off the insects. One directed the forty to fifty onlooking Yaquis. Another acted as circulating nurse. Two of us scrubbed our hands and disinfected them the best we could with alcohol. There was only one pair of sterile rubber gloves so the assistant had to confine himself to what he could do without coming into contact with the site of operation. Meanwhile iodine had been applied on the patient's back. The area to be operated was then thoroughly injected with Novocain, as it was particularly necessary that this patient should feel no pain. As we picked up the scalpel to make the incision there were really some anxious moments. Every surgeon knows that a small foreign body in the deep tissues is often difficult to locate. Without the aid of an X-ray or specially designed instruments, one may cut within a hair's breadth of a bullet and not find it, and repeated cuts near the spine are dangerous. With two score excited Yaqu's looking on at our first operation, it might be just "too bad" if we did not find that bullet. The Lord's favor was with us, the scalpel went true and the bullet was found at once. It was in three fragments. They were dissected out with just enough tissue to hold the three pieces together so that they could be held up for all to see. The murmur of approval that came from that crowd of Yaquis was music to our ears. We dressed the wound and gave Juan a slap on the shoulder to let him know that the operation was over. That he had felt no pain and went on about his business, was a revelation to these men. Juan's recovery was all that could be hoped for. The fee was notable. On learning that we were interested in *guaraches* — the leather sandals universally worn — he brought us a baby pair. We told him that we did not want the shoes off his baby's feet but he answered "feet too big". Since the baby had outgrown the *guaraches,* we were delighted to have them — a most acceptable fee in view of what it meant.

Two days following the time of the first operation, the second governor of Torin asked us to remove a fragment of rock from his neck. He stated that years previously a bullet struck a rock near him and that a fragment of rock lodged in his neck. We could feel it deep in the neck near the jugular vein, but wondered how he could know that it was a rock fragment and not part of a bullet. It caused pain when he swallowed. On opening the neck we found it to be a fragment of rock just as he had stated. He is known among us as "Rock-in-the-neck".

Four other operations were performed during our first say. The last was on the night before we left. The *Fiesta de Gloria,* the great Easter *fiesta,* had come to an end. A young Yaqui attending from a distance, learning that we were leaving the next morning, came about 9 P.M. to ask us to remove a tumor from his eye. The mass was about the size of an egg and overhung the eye, completely obstructing the sight. So we arranged to remove it for him at once. He was placed on a cot in our camp. The audience included the officers of the Mexican garrison and their wives and several soldiers, besides many Yaquis. In addition to the moon light we had an indifferent gasoline torch and two good flash lights. Men with branches fanned away the myriad insects while the operation was performed. The patient was most appreciative as the sight of his eye was restored at once. A friend was instructed about his care and the removal of stitches. In a letter received from our Yaqui interpreter some weeks after our return to the United States there was this welcome information: "I am very glad to write you. Just let you know about the man who you made a operation. Well he thanking you ever so much. He is very well already".

During the second expedition five months later, many came for medical and surgical care. One of the operations performed was somewhat spectacular and especially pleasing to our Yaqui friends. We were asked to see a boy of fourteen who had a growth on his back. We found it to be a cancer and advised the father and mother that the only safe way was to burn it off. They and the boy wanted it done. With a well-equipped operating room, good anaesthetic, capable nurses and an electric cautery it would have been easily done. None of these except the Novocain for local anaesthesia were at hand. An iron rod was found in the door yard and heated in the open fire. The boy was placed on a crude table outside the shelter. The area was injected with Novocain and the red-hot iron applied. The tumor sizzled and smoked as the iron burned it completely away. The boy felt not the least pain, and became at once an object of wonder to his friends.

So much can be done among the Yaquis. They are a courageous, resourceful people. May a wise government soon establish them on lands where they may maintain their homes in security and peace. We look forward to being with them again as one looks forward to a visit with old friends.

Chapter Eight - Physical Characteristics of the Yaqui Indians

Carl Coleman Seltzer

Introduction

In the spring of 1934, the Texas Technological College Yaqui Expedition, under the leadership of Dr. W. C. Holden, was engaged in scientific investigation of the Yaqui Indians of Sonora, Mexico. The writer accompanied the expedition in the capacity of physical anthropologist, [1] and secured a series of anthropometric measurements and observations on a group of 100 adult male members of the tribe.

The Yaquis are an important member of the Cahita division of the Uto-Aztekan linguistic stock, and occupy as their native habitat the lower Rio Yaqui district close to where the river empties into the Gulf of California. Those still living in this region number from 2,500 to 3,000, and reside in the four river villages of Potam, Vicam, Torin and Consica, and in one mountain village, Agua Berde, situated in the Sierra de Bacatete. These groups, however, form merely a small part of the existing population of Yaquis. The majority are widely spread over the western and southern portions of Mexico; there are some even within the United States. What the total population numbers at the present time is very difficult to say. Hrdlička (1), who visited them in 1902, gave an estimate of approximately 20,000, a statement which has been repeatedly affirmed as quite accurate. My own impression is that the number of Yaquis extant today is 12,000 to 15,000. The Yaquis are not a decadent tribe, but one which is being disintegrated slowly but surely by the Mexican government. The reason for this official policy is to be found in the historical resistance of the Yaquis to the dominance and encroachment of their territory and civil liberties by the Spaniards first and then by the Mexicans. Perhaps belligerent by nature, but certainly belligerent in the matter of self-preservation, they have perpetrated the largest series of revolts against the reigning governments that are to be found anywhere in the annals of American Indian tribes. Hrdlička mentions among the numerous uprisings the serious revolts in 1609, 1740-41, 176467, 1825-27, 1832, 1840, 1867-68, 1889-1901, and 1902 (1). Since this time there have been several others, the last one taking place as late as 1927. From the beginning of the twentieth century onwards, the Mexican government has been dealing with this problem in a very clever fashion, by adopting a policy of expatriation and deportation to reduce the number of the Yaquis to a controllable size. Thus within the last fifteen or twenty years, thousands of Yaquis have been moved from their homes along the Rio Yaqui to far distant locations in Yucatan, Tehuantepec and Sinaloa. Some are also living in the neighborhood of Obregon and Hermosillo, as well as in a few of the islands off the west coast of Mexico. Those still living in the Bacatete Mountains have never yet been conquered and are at the present time at war with the government. The United States Yaquis consist of a group of about 200 to 250, and are impounded in a small village called the Barrio Pascua, two miles from the western outskirts of Tucson in Arizona. They are political refugees who escaped from the Mexican army and crossed the border into the United States, after having ambushed a considerable detachment of Mexican soldiers in a box-canyon.

In my series of Yaqui measurements, 17 individuals are included who are members of this Arizona Yaqui colony. The rest were examined by me in the villages of Vicam and Torin. There are a few, however, who come from Potam and Consica. All, so far as could be determined, are considered to be full-bloods. I was permitted to observe only 100 men, as the village chiefs decided that a larger number of measurements, observations, and photographs

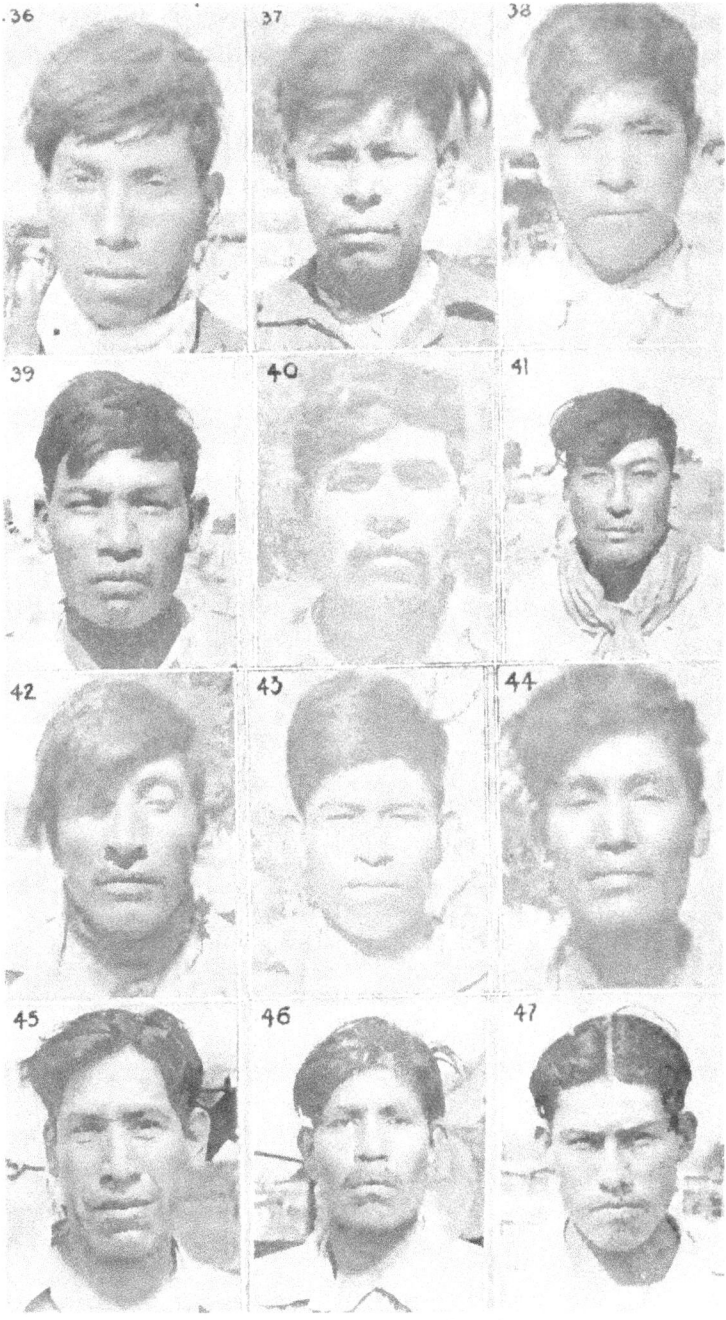

Plate 13 - 36—47. Yaqui facial types.

might be used by the Mexican government as positive means of identification in the event of future outbreaks.

The measurements, a discussion of which follows, were all taken according to the methods embodied in the International Agreement (2), by means of an anthropometer, spreading caliper, sliding caliper and steel tape. Weight was obtained by the use of a bathroom scale, which was found to be very satisfactory for field work. No special instrument was utilized to measure head height, but this feature was obtained by subtracting the standing height to porion from the stature. For skin-color, the Von Luschan scale was found to be fairly satisfactory. Perfect agreements in color matchings, however, were not always possible.

The statistical constants, means, standard deviations, coefficients of variation and probable errors, were all calculated in the usual manner with the assistance of Pearson's table of X_1 and X_2 (3).

Apart from this study, the only other anthropometric observations of the Yaqui Indians were taken by Hrdlička in 1902, as part of his prolific survey for the Hyde Expedition of the American Museum of Natural History, 1898-1903 (4). Unfortunately, only a very small portion of the material obtained has been published so far, consisting up to the present time of means and in some cases dispersion-tables of stature, cephalic index, face height, face breadth, facial index and nasal index, obtained on 50 adult males, and stature measurements on 33 adult females (1). However, many of his valuable physiological and medical observations on the Yaquis have already been made available (4).

Anthropometric Measurements and Proportions

Table 1.   Yaqui Males

	No.	Range	Mean	S. D.	C. V.
Weight (lbs.)	100	81-220	140.70±1.37	20.30	14.43
Stature	100	143-181	166.68±0.44	6.57	3.91
Span	100	158-190	172.20±0.43	6.33	3.68
Relative span	100	96-113	102.94±0.17	2.46	2.39

[2]

The mean weight for Yaqui males is 140.70 pounds. Since the weights recorded include light street clothing, it is estimated that approximately 4 pounds must be subtracted to obtain the mean stripped weight. This still leaves the Yaquis with an average weight which classifies them among the moderately heavy groups of North American Indians.

In stature, the Yaquis also reach moderate dimensions with a mean of 166.68 centimeters (without shoes). This stature considered in conjunction with the average weight indicates, in a rough way, the presence of well-set, solidly built individuals. Hrdlička's measurements (1) give an average stature of 169.6 centimeters for 50 Yaqui males. The difference between his average and that of the present study amounts to about 3 centimeters. This is not a very large divergency, and it may be explained by a variety of reasons. In the first place, there may have been a decrease in stature within the Yaqui tribe in the last thirty years; secondly, shoes worn by the subjects would raise the average considerably; and finally, the smaller size of Hrdlička's series in comparison to the author's might account for the discrepancy. I am inclined to lay most stress on the last possibility, the probability being that Hrdlička's smaller series did not permit so complete a representation of the various villages and localized types.

Span or maximum arm spread is 172.20 centimeters for Yaqui men. The mean excess of span to stature is 5.52 centimeters. This relationship of span to stature is expressed by the relative span index, which is 102.94. The range of 96 to 113 for relative span shows, moreover, that not all the individuals in the series have spans that exceed the statures. There are 6 subjects out of the 100 whose arm spread is less than the measurement of their total body height, indicating the possession by these individuals of relatively shorter arms and narrower shoulders.

Table 2.   Yaqui Males

	No.	Range	Mean	S. D.	C. V.
Sitting height	100	71-91	83.10±0.20	2.91	3.50
Relative sitting height	100	46-55	49.72±0.10	1.54	3.10
Trunk height	100	44-58	51.72±0.17	2.58	4.99
Relative trunk height	100	26-35	30.94±0.11	1.64	5.30

Mean sitting height, which is the measurement of the torso, head and neck, is found to be 83.10 centimeters for the Yaqui males. This is unquestionably a very small average height, especially when the stature of the group is taken into consideration. The author's series of Zuni males (as yet unpublished), with an average stature of 161.43 centimeters, has a mean sitting height of 84.bc, 1.56 centimeters greater than that of the taller Yaquis. This situation is emphasized by the mean relative sitting height (proportion of sitting height to stature) of 49.72 for the Yaquis, in contrast to 52.42 for the Zuñis. For further comparison we find that 20 Sioux described by Hrdlička (5) give a mean relative sitting height of 52.6, and a very large group of Southwestern and Mexican Indians by the same authority (5) shows proportions which average 52.5. It may be said then, that in absolute dimensions and in relative proportions to the total body height, the Yaquis are much smaller in sitting height than many other Indian stocks.

Table 3.   Yaqui Males

	No.	Range	Mean	S. D.	C. V.
Biacromial diameter	100	31-42	37.82±0.12	1.86	4.92
Relative shoulder breadth	100	20-25	22.64±0.06	0.88	3.89
Bi-iliac diameter	100	20-35	29.64±0.13	1.88	6.34
Shoulder-hip index	100	66-93	78.98±0.32	4.76	6.03

Trunk height, the length of the torso alone measured from the sitting position to the supersternal notch, is 51.72 centimeters for Yaqui men. The much smaller Zunis average for the same dimension 53.96 centimeters, 2.24 centimeters greater than the taller Yaquis. It is therefore apparent that the difference between the Yaquis and Zunis is greater in the torso alone, than in the torso, head and neck. The relative trunk height for Yaquis is 30.94 per cent compared to 33.48 per cent for the Zunis. This is additional proof that there is something exceptional in the length of the torso of the Yaquis, the figures indicating a much smaller trunk height relative to stature than is to be found for the Zunis. If we consider all the evidence, then, it is clear that the Yaquis have absolutely and relatively smaller sitting heights than many other Indian groups, and that if we omit the head and neck, and consider the torso alone, a good deal of the proportionate smallness is traceable to this particular dimension.

The Yaquis are not very broad in the shoulders, as indicated by the mean biacromial diameter of 37.82. If the breadth between the shoulders is computed as a percentage of the total stature, this dimension may be described as of moderate width with a definite inclination toward narrowness. In comparison with the Zuñis of New Mexico, the Yaquis are considerably narrower-shouldered relative to stature, with a mean relative shoulder breadth of 22.64 to 23.16 for the Zuñis.

In the breadth between the hips the Yaquis attain a mean dimension of 29.64 centimeters. We find a higher variability for this diameter than for shoulder width, the coefficient of variation of hip breadth being 6.34 to 4.92 for the shoulders. When the biiliac diameter is considered as a percentage of the shoulder width, we obtain the high mean index value of 78.98. The Yaquis, then, have broad hips relative to the width of their shoulders. The Zuñis for the same proportions give a mean index of 75.58. The latter are accordingly much narrower in the hips relative to the shoulders than the Yaqu's. The variation in this index is fairly high, the coefficient of variation being 6.03 and the range 66 to 93.

Table 4.   Yaqui Males

	No.	Range	Mean	S. D.	C. V.
Chest breadth	100	23-34	27.87±0.12	1.83	6.57
Chest depth	100	16-25	21.38±0.12	1.78	8.33
Thoracic index	100	67-90	76.78±0.31	4.60	5.93

The breadth (lateral) and the depth (antero-posterior) dimensions of the chest were taken as a mean between inspiration and expiration, at about the level of the nipples. In comparison to the smaller Zuñis, the Yaquis have practically the same chest breadth, but are considerably greater in the depth of the chest. But in contrast to Hrdlička's Indians of the Southwest and Mexico (5), the Yaquis have not only narrower chests but also shallower chest diameters. The mean chest breadth for Yaqui males is 27.87 centimeters and for

Hrdlička's Indians 29.9 centimeters. The mean chest depth for Yaquis is computed to be 21.38 centimeters against 22.8 centimeters for Hrdlička's Indians. In regard, however, to the relative proportion of the chest dimensions, as indicated by the thoracic index, the Yaquis are very similar to Hrdlička's Indians of the Southwest and Mexico, with a mean of 76.78 for the author's series and 76.15 for the latter group. Thus, in comparison with many other Indian tribes, the Yaquis have smaller chest dimensions, but similar chest proportions. And if we recall that the Yaqui had considerably shorter sitting heights, this tendency being particularly apparent in the torso, it is highly probable that they are also comparatively shorter in the length of the rib cage.

Table 5.	Yaqui Males				
	No.	Range	Mean	S. D.	C. V.
Upper arm length	100	28-39	32.68±0.13	1.93	6.00
Lower arm length	100	21-34	25.44±0.13	1.93	7.70
Lower leg length	100	28-45	38.38±0.16	2.34	6.10

Upper arm length is the distance from the acromion to the superior head of the radius. Lower arm length represents the length of the radius itself, from its superior head to the distal end of the styloid process of the same bone. Lower leg length is the total longitudinal length of the tibia, measured from the medial aspect of the superior border of the condyles to the distal edge of the medial malleolus.

The means of these dimensions among the male Yaquis deserve no special comment. When, however, the proportion of lower arm length to upper arm length is calculated, by the index of the means, this figure, 77.84, does indicate the possession by the Yaquis of comparatively greater lower arm segments relative to the upper arm length than is commonly found among many groups.

Table 6	Yaqui Males				
	No.	Range	Mean	S. D.	C. V.
Head circumference	100	490-594	546.20±0.98	14.75	2.63
Head length	100	167-202	183.84±0.43	6.42	3.49
Head breadth	100	135-161	149.23±0.34	4.98	3.31
Cephalic index	100	72-92	81.28±0.27	3.96	4.87

The size of the Yaqui head, as indicated by the mean circumference of 546.20 millimeters, is relatively small. Even the Zunis of New Mexico, who weigh less than the Yaquis and are much shorter in stature, have a head circumference which is slightly higher than this series. Further confirmation of this comparative smallness of the Yaqui cranium can be had on the calculation of the cranial module. From the average of the means of the length, breadth and height of the head, one computes an average cephalic module of

153.7. Hrdlička (5) gives an average cephalic module of 164.0 for his male Sioux, and a minimum index of 155.7. The Sioux head is known for its large size; nevertheless, the Yaqui average does not come up to the size of even the smallest Sioux cranium.

The Yaquis of this series are not entirely free from artificial deformation of the head. About one-third of the group shows some signs of flattening in the occipital region. It is most often very flight in amount, however, and does not modify the original diameters to any great extent. The Yaquis have a very short head length (183.84 mm.) and a head breadth of moderate dimensions. The undeformed head length probably runs around 185 millimeters. The mean cephalic index of 81.28 places the Yaquis in the upper limits of the mesocephalic class. The cephalic index of the undeformed individuals is 80.65, from which the reader may gather that artificial deformation among this group of Yaquis does not effect any serious modification of the cranial proportions. Hrdlička (1) has presented a dispersion table for the cephalic index of 49 Yaqui males, all undeformed heads. From this table I have computed an average index of 78.6 for his series. The latter group then are more dolecocephalic than the Yaquis of this study.

Table 7.   Yaqui Males

	No.	Range	Mean	S. D.	C. V.
Head height	100	109-158	128.05±0.59	8.70	6.79
Length-height index	100	57-83	69.91±0.31	4.65	6.65
Breadth-height index	100	68-99	85.54±0.43	6.32	7.39

The head height mean of 128.05 millimeters for Yaqui males is fairly high. The series, however, is not very uniform in this respect. It exhibits an extraordinary amount of variability for this measurement, as can be seen from the range of 109-158 and the standard deviation of 8.70. Although in absolute dimensions the Yaqui head presents a well-elevated vault, it should be described as moderate in relation to its length and specially in relation to its breadth. The mean length-height index of 69.91 is considerably lower than Hrdlička's Indians of the Southwest and Mexico (72.2), but still relatively higher than his Chippewa and Sioux. When the height is expressed as a percentage of the breadth, the Yaquis become much lower-headed indeed. Their mean index of 85.54 is below that of Hrdlička's Indians of the Southwest and Mexico (89.7), his Chippewa (87.2) and Sioux (86.3). The Yaquis, then, are characterized by a head height which is of good elevation in absolute dimensions, but in proportion to its length and breadth is much lower than many other American Indian groups.

Table 8.   Yaqui Males

	No.	Range	Mean	S. D.	C. V.
Minimum frontal diameter	100	85-116	100.78±0.40	5.92	5.87
Fronto-parietal index	100	55-75	67.70±0.25	3.72	5.49

One of the outstanding features of the Yaqui head is the narrowness of the forehead as expressed by the minimum frontal diameter. It is much narrower than the mean frontal breadth of the Zunis, as well as of most of the other Southwestern and Mexican tribes. The relationship of the minimum frontal diameter to the maximum head breadth is given by the fronto-parietal index. The size of this index in Yaqui males indicates a skull vault which, although it is quite narrow in the front, expands very rapidly as one goes backwards toward the parietal and occipital regions. It is a very narrow forehead in relation to the width of the head.

Table 9. Yaqui Males

	No.	Range	Mean	S. D.	C. V.
Maximum bizygomatic diameter	100	120-159	141.00±0.39	5.85	4.15
Cephalo-facial index	100	81-107	94.18±0.28	4.05	4.34
Zygo-frontal index	100	56-95	72.06±0.33	4.96	6.88

The Yaqui men are quite narrow in facial width, especially so for an American Indian group. They are much smaller in this dimension than the average of the Southwestern and Mexican Indians. Our mean of 141 millimeters agrees almost exactly with the average bizygomatic diameter obtained by Hrdlička in 1902 for the same group.

The ratio of width of face to width of head, as expressed by the cephalo-facial index, is particularly useful in estimating the degree of white mixture present in an Indian tribe. When the index is low it is indicative of a considerable admixture of non-Indian stock, for in Indian and white mixtures, the index falls usually as a result of a larger decrease in face breadth than head breadth (6). Among the Yaquis, however, a mean index of 94.18 is high enough to rule out any appreciable admixture of non-Indian stock.

The mean zygo-frontal index for Yaqui males suggests a normal proportion of face width to forehead breadth.

Table 10. Yaqui Males

	No.	Range	Mean	S. D.	C. V.
Bi-ocular diameter	100	79-102	92.83±0.29	4.28	4.61
Inter-ocular diameter	100	30-43	35.78±0.17	2.56	7.15

The bi-ocular diameter represents the maximum distance between the external palpebral margins of the eyes. It is a measurement which is very seldom taken but which has, in many instances, considerable value. In Yaqui males, this dimension indicates a relatively wide set of the eyes in respect to the width of the face and particularly so in regard to the breadth of the forehead. The mean bi-ocular diameter for the Yaquis is larger than that of the Zunis, even though the latter have broader faces and larger frontal breadths than the Yaquis.

Table 11.   Yaqui Males

	No.	Range	Mean	S. D.	C. V.
Total face height	100	105-149	127.50±0.44	6.50	5.10
Total facial index	100	75-104	90.20±0.35	5.15	5.71
Upper facial height	100	60-84	73.20±0.34	5.10	6.97
Upper facial index	100	43-63	52.10±0.24	2.54	6.73

The inter-ocular diameter is the breadth between the eyes, measured from the internal canthic margins. This dimension again substantiates the fact that the eyes of the Yaquis are set wide apart in relation to other proportions of the face.

The length of the face, measured from nasion to menton, is 127.50 millimeters for the Yaqui men of this study. Hrdlička (1) obtained an average menton-nasion height of 120.9 millimeters for 52 Yaqui males. There is, therefore, a discrepancy of more than 6 millimeters between our measurements. I find it very difficult to account for so marked a disagreement. It is hardly possible that it is the result of an actual increase in this dimension among the Yaquis within a generation or more. If this were the case, one would expect to find correlative increases in other features such as stature, nose height, et cetera. But as we have seen there is no such increase in stature. I am rather inclined to believe that the disparity is partly due to differences in technique used by the investigators, in the location of the nasion point on the living. We have a measure of comparison of what the actual menton-nasion height was at the time Hrdlička gathered his material, in a series of male crania 11 in number. [3] The mean mention-nasion height for these skulls, which must be accurate, is 123.3 millimeters, more than 3 millimeters larger than the same measurement on the living. If we add at least 2 millimeters for the flesh difference to make it representative of the menton-nasion height on the living, we obtain the figure of 125.3. This reconstructed result is much closer to my mean of 127.50 than to Hrdlička's average of 120.9.

Total facial index, the relation of the length of the face to its width, gives a leptoprosopic or a relatively long-faced ratio in the Yaquis. Hrdlička's shortened face height would make his series almost euryprosopic.

The length of the upper face from nasion to prosthion is 73.20 millimeters in the male Yaquis. This is merely a moderate upper face height in proportion to the total length of the face, but relative to the breadth it gives the Yaquis a comparatively long and narrow upper facial index.

Table 12   Yaqui Males

	No.	Range	Mean	S. D.	C. V.
Bigonial diameter	100	94-125	109.10±0.38	5.56	5.10
Fronto-gonial index	100	91-130	108.90±0.51	7.60	6.98
Zygo-gonial index	100	67-87	77.60±0.23	3.48	4.48
Jaw length	100	80-124	104.80±0.46	6.90	6.58

The breadth of the lower jaw between the two gonial angles is very large in Yaquis, especially when considered in relation to other important facial dimensions. It is larger in this group than similar diameters of the Zunis and Hrdlička's Southwestern and Mexican tribes, but somewhat smaller than the bigonial breadths of the larger-faced Sioux and Chippewa.

The fronto-gonial index for the Yaquis of 108.90 and the zygo-gonial index of 77.60 are very high, and indicate an exceptionally broad jaw relative to the width of forehead and breadth of face. These ratios are much larger in Yaquis than in Zuñis and Southwestern and Mexican Indians, the latter groups having much narrower jaws in proportion to their diameters of forehead and face. Jaw length is the distance from the left gonion to symphysion, the midpoint on the chin which marks the junction of the two halves of the mandible. Although this dimension is not the true projective length of the jaw, being more accurately the length of the lower border of the horizontal ramus, from it, with the use of the bigonial diameter, we can actually compute in a rough way, the "true" or projected jaw length. This can be done by considering one-half of the bigonial diameter as the base of a right triangle, and the gonion-symphysion length as its hypotenuse. The height of the triangle will be, of course, the "true" length of the lower jaw. Using this method I have computed this dimension to be 89.2 millimeters. This figure, considered together with the mean jaw length of 104.8 millimeters, indicates a jaw which is short in absolute dimensions as well as in proportion to its breadth. The Zunis, who have a much smaller jaw breadth, exhibit a larger jaw length (105.50) and a greater projected length (90.9).

Table 13.   Yaqui Males

	No.	Range	Mean	S. D.	C. V.
Nose height	100	44-63	55.02±0.25	3.76	6.83
Nose breadth	100	34-51	42.29±0.23	3.42	8.09
Nasal index	100	60-95	77.38±0.46	6.76	8.74
Nose salient	100	16-26	20.99±0.13	1.98	9.19

The nose of the Yaquis is moderately long but rather broad. The mean nasal index of 77.38 places this group in the messorrhine class. There is considerable variation in this feature, however, for although more than half of the individuals in the series have messorrhine noses, the others are about equally divided between leptorrhine and platyrrhine divisions. Hrdlička's Yaquis (1) have a higher mean nasal index (78.96) than the Yaquis of this study. This is probably accountable by the fact that Hrdlička located his nasion point lower than this investigator, thereby obtaining a shorter nasal height, and a resultant higher index. The 12 Yaqui skulls measured by Hrdlička give an average nasal index of 50.3. This index on the skull is in the upper limits of messorrhiny, approaching very closely a platyrrhine classification.

Nose salient represents the distance from the tip of the nose to the junction of the septum with the upper lip. It is not a very accurate measurement, but it does give in a general way the extent of the projection of the nose from the face. The mean for this dimension in the Yaquis is 20.99 millimeters, and indicates a nose that stands out very prominently from the facial skeleton. It is a much more prominent nose at the tip than that of the Zunis, whose mean nose salient is but 19.46 millimeters.

The observations on the color of the skin were taken by means of a Von Luschan color scale. The color of the forehead was chosen to represent the exposed or tanned portion of the skin, while the inner surface of the arm was taken to represent the unexposed surface. From the frequencies of the color

Skin

	Skin Color Forehead		Skin Color Inner Arm		Vascularity	
Von Luschan Scale	No.	%	No.	%	Absent	No. 100	% 100.00
Red brown (12-14, 16)	2	2.00	11	11.00		
Light brown (15, 17, 18)	8	8.00	19	19 00		
Yellow brown (19, 20, 6)	12	12.00	32	32.00		
Medium brown (21-25)	46	46.00	36	36.00		
Chocolate (26-29)	32	32.00	2	2.00		
	100		100			

Freckles	No.	%	Moles	No.	%
Absent	98	98.00	Absent	40	40.82
Few	2	2.00	Few	52	53.06
			Many	6	6.12
	100			98	

categories in the above tables, it may be seen that the Yaquis are, as a whole, relatively dark-skinned. They are more heavily pigmented than most of the North American Indian groups, and in this respect are comparable to the Pimas of Arizona. More than one-third of the Yaquis have unexposed skin colors which match Nos. 21-25 on the Von Luschan scale, a color range which is decidedly negroid in its degree of intensity. The exposed or tanned surface as represented by the color of the forehead, is predominantly of this heavily pigmented negroid type, with 46 per cent of the series in the medium brown division (Nos. 21-25) and 32 per cent in the chocolate classification (Nos. 26-29). Thus, it is clear that the Yaquis besides having a natural tendency toward the dark skin colors, are very susceptible to tanning on exposure to the rays of the sun.

Vascularity of the skin, observed as to the presence and absence of normal surface hyperemia, is completely absent in the Yaquis of this study. Freckles, a feature which is usually found among lighter-skinned peoples and groups of mixed origin, are virtually absent among the Yaquis. Moles, however, are relatively common among the more heavily pigmented races, and in the Yaquis more than one-half of the series show this characteristic to a moderate degree. A pronounced number of moles is present in only 6.12 per cent of individuals.

Yaqui head hair is almost invariably straight. There were but two individuals whose hair fell into the low wave classification, and one whose hair form was characterized as deep-waved. The texture of the hair is predominantly fine to medium, coarse hair being practically absent in the Yaquis.

Observations were taken on the quantity of the hair on the head, face and body. The head hair shows a heavy or thick development with 48 per cent of the group in this particular category. The Yaquis have very slightly developed

Hair

Hair Form	No.	%	Hair Texture	No.	%	Head Hair Quantity	No.	%
Straight	97	97.00	Coarse	7	7.00	Thin	4	4.00
Low waves	2	2.00	Medium	25	25.00	Medium	48	48.00
Deep waves	1	1.00	Fine	68	68.00	Thick	48	48.00
	100			100			100	

Baldness	No.	%	Beard Quantity	No.	%	Body Hair Quantity	No.	%
Absent	98	98.00	Very sparse	69	69.00			
Slight	1	1.00	Sparse	22	22.00	Absent	99	99.00
			Moderate	8	8.00			
Moderate	1	1.00	Pronounced	1	1.00	Slight	1	1.00
	100			100			100	

Hair Color Head	No.	%	Head Hair Color Variation	No.	%	Grayness Head	No.	%
						Absent	78	78.00
Black	100	100.00	Dark brown			Slight	13	13.00
			sheen	15	15.31	Moderate	4	4.00
			Jet black	83	84.69	Pronounced	5	5.00
				98			100	

Grayness Beard	No.	%	Eyebrow Thickness	No.	%	Eyebrow Concurrency	No.	%
Absent	83	83.00	Submedium	32	32.00			
Slight	10	10.00	Medium	53	53.00	Absent	83	83.00
			Pronounced	12	12.00			
Moderate	3	3.00	Very			Slight	16	16.00
Pronounced	4	4.00	Pronounced	3	3.00	Moderate	1	1.00
	100			100			100	

face hair, however, more than 90 per cent of their numbers exhibiting very sparse or sparse beards. The possession of a mustache is a relatively common phenomenon in this tribe, but rarely shows itself as a heavy growth. And finally, the Yaquis approach the mongoloid lack of corporeal hirsuteness, with all but one individual of the series showing a complete absence of body hair. The color of the hair when observed lying flat on the head is black in every single instance. But when the hair is held up directly toward the source of light, 15.31 per cent of the series display a dark brown sheen, the rest remaining jet black even under this test. Accordingly, it may be said that the Yaquis have really darker hair than the Zunis, who show a higher percentage of the "dark brown sheen" type.

Baldness is extraordinarily rare among the Yaquis, while graying of the head hair and beard hair is moderately common. The eyebrows are medium to submedium in degree of thickness, with the pronouncedly thick type present in 12 per cent of the series. Concurrent eyebrows are absent in the majority of cases. When the characteristic is present, it is almost invariably very slightly developed.

Eyes

Eye Color	No.	%	Eye Opening Height	No.	%	Internal Eyefolds	No.	%
Black	53	53.00	Submedium	37	37.00	Absent	91	91.92
Dark			Medium	58	58.00	Submedium	5	5.05
						Medium	4	3.03
Brown	47	47.00	Pronounced	5	5.00	Pronounced	0	0.00
	100			100			99	

Median Eyefolds	No.	%	External Eyefolds	No.	%	Eye Obliquity	No.	%
Absent	66	66.00	Absent	64	64.00	Absent	6	6.00
Submedium	24	24.00	Submedium	11	11.00	Slight	57	57.00
Medium	4	4.00	Medium	10	10.00	Medium	29	29.00
Pronounced	6	6.00	Pronounced	15	15.00	Pronounced	8	8.00
	100			100			100	

Perhaps the most significant feature recorded for Yaqui eyes is the surprisingly large percentage of black eye color. Eyes are said to be black when the color of the iris is as dark as the pupil itself. Fifty-three per cent of the Yaquis present this degree of iris pigmentation, in contrast to 47 per cent of the black and brown variety for the rest of the series. Black eyes, observed according to the above distinction for this category of eye color, are rather rare in many North American Indian groups. Among the Zunis, it is found in only a fraction of one per cent of the total male series. Similar negligible proportions are to be seen in the Hopis and Navajos as well. Black eyes are to be found as a distinctive feature in Negroes and Negroids and accordingly, its large representation in the Yaqui population is unquestionably significant.

The height of the opening of the lids of the eyes is medium to submedium in the Yaqui males. This narrowness between the palpebral margins is probably due to the glare of the sunlight, resulting in characteristic squinting eyes. Internal or Mongoloid eyefolds are relatively rare in this tribe, with less than 10 per cent of the group showing any signs of its presence at all. The median and external epicanthic folds, however, are substantially represented, the latter type being found in a more developed condition than the median form. Pronounced external eyefolds are present in 15 per cent of individuals, a medium-sized eyefold in 10 per cent and the small variety in 11 per cent.

The outer corner of the eye almost always shows some form of upward tilt or obliquity. A slight obliquity is by far the most usual occurrence, with a moderate degree of upward slant having the next largest frequency.

Forehead and Temporal Region

Forehead Height	No.	%	Forehead Slope	No.	%	Browridges	No.	%
Low	4	4.00	Absent	13	13.00	Small	11	11.00
Medium	66	66.00	Slight	46	46.00	Medium	31	31.00
High	30	30.00	Moderate	35	35.00	Large	43	43.00
			Pronounced	5	5.00	Very large	15	15.00
	100		Very pronounced	1	1.00			
				100			100	

Temporal Fullness	No.	%
Submedium	72	72.00
Medium	24	24.00
Pronounced	4	4.00
	100	

The observations on the height of the forehead concur with the head height measurement. The prevailing form is a forehead of medium height, with a frequent representation of the high variety. Low frontal regions are found in only 4 per cent of cases. The slope of the forehead is not very pronounced in the Yaquis. It is most commonly slight or moderate in its degree of backward inclination.

The Yaquis are characterized by the possession of large browridges. Small supraorbital ridges are present in but 11 per cent of individuals, while the large or very large types are to be found in more than half of the series.

A submedium degree of temporal fullness or flat temples is the most predominant form, 72 per cent of the Yaquis falling into this category. There is no close correlation in this series between the degree of temporal fullness and the nutritive condition of the subjects.

The Yaqui nose presents a number of very interesting features. In addition to evidences of unusual variability in certain characteristics especially in the nasal root and bridge, one is impressed by the irregularity of the combinations of these features in the same population.

Nose

Nasion Depression

	No.	%
Absent	6	6.06
Very small	16	16.16
Small	13	13.13
Medium	46	46.46
Pronounced	17	17.17
Very pronounced	1	1.01
	99	

Nasal Root Height

	No.	%
Very low	1	1.00
Low	10	10.00
Medium	59	59.00
High	26	26.00
Very high	4	4.00
	100	

Nasal Root Breadth

	No.	%
Very narrow	11	11.00
Narrow	15	15.00
Medium	59	59.00
Broad	13	13.00
Very broad	2	2.00
	100	

Nasal Bridge Height

	No.	%
Low	2	2.00
Medium	29	29.00
High	53	53.00
Very high	16	16.00
	100	

Nasal Bridge Breadth

	No.	%
Narrow	5	5.00
Medium	64	64.00
Broad	30	30.00
Very broad	1	1.00
	100	

Nasal Profile

	No.	%
Concave	2	2.00
Concave-snub	0	0.00
Straight	6	6.00
Straight-snub	7	7.00
Convex	52	52.00
Convex-snub	33	33.00
	100	

Nasal Tip Thickness

	No.	%
Submedium	8	8.00
Medium	81	81.00
Pronounced	11	11.00
	100	

Nasal Tip Inclination

	No.	%
Up moderately	11	11.00
Up slightly	73	73.00
Horizontal	9	9.00
Down slightly	6	6.00
Down moderately	1	1.00
	100	

Nasal Septum

	No.	%
Straight & concave	3	3.00
Convex	97	97.00
	100	

Nasal Wings

	No.	%
Compressed	2	2.00
Medium	13	13.00
Flaring	85	85.00
	100	

Nostrils Frontal Visibility

	No.	%
Absent	14	14.00
Slight & moderate	67	67.00
Pronounced	19	19.00
	100	

Nostrils Lateral Visibility

	No.	%
Absent	11	11.22
Present	87	88.78
	98	

Nostrils Shape

	No.	%
Thin	2	2.00
Medium	97	97.00
Round	1	1.00
	100	

Nostrils Axes

	No.	%
Slightly oblique	26	26.53
Moderately oblique	72	73.47
	98	

If we consider the nasion depression first, we find that a Yaqui may show almost any degree of depression in this region. In more than 22 per cent of cases, the nasion depression may be completely absent or very small, it may be small in 13 per cent of individuals and pronounced or very pronounced in more than 18 per cent of cases. The height of the nasal root is predominantly medium to high, yet in more than 10 per cent of the series it is decidedly low. In the breadth of the nasal root, the Yaquis are most commonly medium to narrow; the broad and very broad types however, are present in 15 per cent of subjects. When we come to the question of the nasal bridge, we encounter a more uniform picture. The nasal bridge is prevailingly high, and in width it is medium to broad. Low and narrow bridges of the nose are quite rare.

In the observation of the nasal profile, an artificial division was made with respect to the bony and cartilaginous portions of the nose. When the fleshy and cartilaginous section of the profile in the region of the nasal tip was raised above the continuation of the original bony profile, then such a nose was characterized as snub. In the Yaquis, a snub condition of the nose was observed in 40 per cent of cases. This is indicative of the presence in the Yaquis of a well-developed fleshy nasal tip. Concave nasal profiles are very uncommon in this group, and the concave-snub form entirely absent. The straight type is found in only 6 per cent of individuals, and the straight variety with a little rise near tire nasal tip (straight-snub) is present in 7 per cent of the series. The characteristic nasal profile is a convex one with a snub tip almost as frequently present as it is absent. In many instances, however, the degree of convexity to be seen was very slight indeed.

Lips

Lips: Integumental Thickness	No.	%
Thin	3	3.00
Medium	33	33.00
Pronounced	64	64.00
	100	

Lips: Membranous Thickness	No.	%
Submedium	2	2.00
Medium	31	31.00
Pronounced	50	50.00
Very pronounced	17	17.00
	100	

Lips: Eversion	No.	%
Submedium	13	13.00
Medium	46	46.00
Pronounced	22	22.00
Very pronounced	19	19.00
	100	

Lip Seam	No.	%
Absent	52	52.00
Small	18	18.00
Moderate	21	21.00
Pronounced	9	9.00
	100	

The thickness of the nasal tip is medium to pronounced, and its inclination decidedly upwards. A downward tilt of the nasal tip is found in only 7 per cent of the individuals. The profile of the nasal septum is almost invariably convex, and the spread of the nasal wings has been designated as flaring in by far the majority of instances.

In association with the upward tilt of the nasal tip, we find a good frontal and lateral exposure of the nostrils. The shape of the nasal openings is in practically every case medium, not thin or round. And finally, the axes of the nostrils are preponderantly moderately oblique.

We now come to a feature in which the Yaquis display their greatest individuality. It is in the lips that they present their most persistent unconformity to the orthodox and characteristic configuration of the North American Indian.

Face

Alveolar Prognathism

	No.	%
Absent	58	58.00
Slight	28	28.00
Moderate	10	10.00
Pronounced	3	3.00
Very pronounced	1	1.00
	100	

Mid-facial Prognathism

	No.	%
Absent	92	92.92
Slight	7	7.07
	99	

Malars Frontal Projection

	No.	%
Absent & submedium	64	64.00
Medium	29	29.00
Pronounced	7	7.00
	100	

Malars Lateral Projection

	No.	%
Absent	1	1.00
Submedium	38	38.00
Medium	29	29.00
Pronounced	26	26.00
Very pronounced	6	6.00
	100	

Chin Prominence

	No.	%
Submedium	51	51.00
Medium	47	47.00
Pronounced	2	2.00
	100	

Gonial Angles

	No.	%
Submedium	22	22.22
Medium	60	60.60
Pronounced	16	16.16
Very pronounced	1	1.01
	99	

Chin Type

	No.	%
Median	87	95.60
Bilateral	4	4.40
	91	

The thickness of the integumental portions of the lips is pronounced in as much as 64 per cent of individuals. The membranous division of the lips is pronouncedly or very pronouncedly thick in 67 per cent of cases, and thin in only 2 out of 100 subjects. Not only are the lips very full and thick, but they also show a large percentage of above-average eversion. Pronouncedly everted lips are found in 22 per cent of Yaquis and the very pronounced type in 19 per cent. A submedium eversion of the lips is seen in only 13 out of 100 individuals. The lip seam, which refers to the lighter raised line marking the boundary between the integumental and membranous portions of the lips, is present in almost half of the members of the series. Its most predominant form is a moderate development, with the pronounced type present in 9 per cent of instances.

There is, therefore, an element in the Yaqui population which possesses decidedly negroid lips, lips which are thick, everted, and show a definite lip seam. Such features cannot conceivably have appeared in the population individually, as a matter of chance. There is no doubt that they are all closely linked together, and it is probable that their presence in the Yaqui tribe should be accounted for on a strictly racial basis.

Prognathism among the Yaquis is predominantly of the alveolar type. Mid-facial prognathism is found only in 7 per cent of cases. Almost half of the series, however, shows some degree of protrusiveness of the alveolar region; in most cases this is not very marked but rather slight in its development.

Ears

Ears: Roll of Helix	No.	%	Ears: Darwin's Points	No.	%	Antihelix	No.	%
Very slight	7	7.00	Absent	91	91.00	Absent	1	1.00
Slight	25	25.00	Small	5	5.00	Small	36	36.00
Moderate	67	67.00	Medium	3	3.00	Medium	61	61.00
Pronounced	1	1.00	Large	1	1.00	Pronounced	2	2.00
	100			100			100	

Ear Lobe	No.	%		Ear Lobe, Size	No.	%
Soldered	7	7.00	Small		14	14.00
Attached	36	36.00	Medium		60	60.00
Free	57	57.00	Large		26	26.00
	100				100	

Ears: Protrusion	No.	%		Ear Slant	No.	%
Slight	22	22.00	Medium		97	97.00
Medium	68	68.00				
Pronounced	10	10.00	Pronounced		3	3.00
	100				100	

The Yaquis display a moderate frontal projection of the malars. Thirty-six per cent show a medium or pronounced malar projection, and practically all of the absent and submedium clas-5 if separated would be submedium. Thus the Yaquis have more projecting malars than "Europeans" or Whites, who, according to my classification, would present principally an absence of frontal malar prominence. The Yaquis approach more closely the mongoloid and negroid conditions of this feature. In lateral projection of the malars, the Yaquis are quite variable. There is a large percentage of individuals with a submedium development of the zygomatic arches (38 p.c.), and an almost equally large group with the pronounced or very pronounced forms (32 p.c.).

The prominence of the chin is observed as submedium when its most anterior projection is behind the lines of the frontal facial angle, and pronounced if it projects in front of it. On the basis of the frequencies of the divisional categories given in the table of mandibular prominence, the Yaqui chin may be said to be on the whole slightly receding. Pronouncedly prominent chins are very rare. The Yaqui chin is more protrusive than that of the Zunis, whose submedium class is 25 per cent larger than the Indians of this study.

The gonial angles of the lower jaw are quite prominent, particularly so in relation to the line of the lateral facial angle. A submedium condition of the gonial angles is present in only 22.22 per cent of the individuals.

The roll of the helix of the ear is moderate to slight, and the development of the antihelix is similarly medium to small. The appearance of a Darwin's point is very infrequent in the Yaquis, with less than 10 per cent of the group showing any signs of its presence whatsoever. A medium-sized ear lobe is the usual condition, and its relationship to the side of the head is found to be more often free than attached. The ears of the Yaquis are moderately protrusive, more so in this tribe than in the Zunis, where the ears lie closer to the side of the head. Pronouncedly slanting ears are very uncommon.

Occipital Region

Occipital Protrusion			Cranial Deformation		
	No.	%		No.	%
Absent	37	37.00	Absent	62	62.00
			Occipital small	25	25.00
Slight	60	60.00	Occipital moderate	10	10.00
Moderate	3	3.00	Occipital pronounced	3	3.00
	100			100	

The typical form of the occiput in the Yaquis is one in which there is a slight protrusion. It is highly probable that such a condition would still remain the dominant form in spite of the practice of artificial deformation. Cranial deformation is entirely absent in 62 per cent of individuals. It can be observed, when present, as a slight to moderate flattening in the occipital region. Its effect upon the cranial diameters does not assume serious proportions.

In general body build, the Yaquis are usually slender or moderately

General Body Build

	No.	%
Linear	57	57.00
Medium	35	35.00
Lateral	8	8.00
	100	

proportioned. There is perhaps a greater tendency towards the linear condition than to the fatter configuration. The Yaquis are judged to be more heavily built or more thick-set than the Zunis, whose frequency of the linear form amounts to as much as 72.99 per cent of the total male series.

Remarks

It must be apparent to the reader, from the study of the measurements and observations, that the Yaqui Indians do not form a very homogeneous population. Some physical types are shown in Plate 13. Throughout the analysis of the individual features, we have pointed out numerous instances of unusual variability, as evidenced by the range, distribution, and cases of multimodal dispersions in certain of the characters. This extensive variability referred to is not indicative of a natural or original multiform condition in the Yaqui tribe, but is, on the contrary, unquestionably traceable to the admixture of these people with a number of other Indian stocks, in addition to the more or less recent acquisition of small quantities of non-Indian blood. This heterogeneity was clearly observable to the writer while examining the subjects in the field. He was quickly impressed by the number and diversity of the types that appeared within the population. The segregation of these types, their identification, and the establishment of the extent of their participation in the composition of the group, presents a very complex and difficult problem. Its complete solution will certainly necessitate a larger series of measurements than heretofore obtained.

There are, however, certain impressions or indications which point to the relationships of several of these types with neighboring tribes in the northwestern Mexican district. The most important of these would be with the Mayo, Opata, Seri and Pima. There is evidence in the literature for the historical intermixture of the Yaquis with the above stocks. It is extremely difficult to say how much of the type resemblances between the Yaquis and these other groups may be due to the factor of miscegnation or to basic affiliations through common origin. Nevertheless, it does seem highly probable that the Yaqui-Piman relationship is a fundamentally close one. Hrdlička (1) has already drawn attention to this fact, and has further suggested that "The Yaquis are apparently a Pima physical stock, modified by mixture with the Mayos". Inasmuch as no detailed comparison between the Yaquis and Pimas has been made with respect to a large series of physical characteristics, confirmation of this assertion must necessarily be temporarily withheld. The final decision in regard to this matter will have to wait until there is available a more modern and thorough investigation of the Pima tribe than any we have at the present time.

The determination of the physical status and consanguineous derivations and alliances of the Yaquis, is of course, of first importance. To the physical anthropologist, however, these inquiries become of lesser significance when we discover that this group may present unique suggestions relative to the larger and more comprehensive problems of the American Indian. It is possible that here we may find notable collateral evidence relating to the origin and composition of the American Indian as a racial unit. Pertinent suggestions under this head appear in the presence in the Yaqui population of a number of negroid features. The most explicit of these characters have been already pointed out in the presentation of material. They are, in general, more prevalent in the soft parts of the body than in the skeletal parts. A list of the morphological observations which illustrate definite tendencies as well as approximations to negroid features includes the possession by the Yaquis of a relatively dark skin color, one which is darker than most groups of Indians; a significantly large quantity of "jet black" hair even when held up to the light; a large percentage of really black eyes; a heavy development of the browridges; a preponderance of flaring nasal wings; a very high degree of frontal visibility of the nostrils; an unusual frequency of broad nasal bridges; and the repeated occurrence of a retrogressive chin. But unquestionably, the most significantly exponential features are in the lips. For here we meet with a group of individuals with lips of such a pronounced thickness, with so marked a degree of eversion, together with so prominent a development of the lip seam, that other than a negroid classification for these characteristics would be unsuitable. In metric measurements and indices this association is not so clear. Nevertheless, the Yaquis do show in comparison with many other Indian tribes, a relatively shorter trunk, longer arms, longer legs, a large breadth of the nose, and in quite a few instances a platyrrhine nasal index.

It is not the purpose of the writer to enter into any great detail with respect to this problem at the present time. But it does seem evident that there is an element in the Yaqui population with a strong suggestion of certain negroid features. What is now most pertinent is to discover where and particularly when this element entered the group. Is it a somewhat recent admixture in the postColumbian period with Negroes or Negroids as the case may be, or is it something of more ancient and fundamental composition? The answer to this question must take the form, in great part, of an exhaustive inquiry into the historical post-Columbian literature of northwestern Mexico. It is the intention of the author to embody the outcome of his analysis as well as that of other correlative problems, in the near future, in a final report on the racial origin and composition of this important group.

Peabody Museum,
Harvard University, January, 1935

Bibliography

(1) Hrdlička, A. 1904. "The Indians of Sonora, Mexico." *American Anthropologist,* new series, volume 6, pp. 51-89.

(2) Hrdlička, A. 1920. *Anthropometry.* Wistar Institute.

(3) Pearson, K. 1914. *Tables for Statisticians and Biometricians.*

(4) Hrdlička, A. 1915. Physiological and Medical Observations among the Indians of Southwestern United States and Northern Mexico. *Bureau of American Ethnology, bulletin, 34.*

(5) Hrdlička, A. 1931. "Anthropology of the Sioux." *American Journal of Physical Anthropology*, volume 16, number 2, pp. 123-166.

(6) Seltzer, C. C. 1933. "The Anthropometry of the Western and Copper Eskimos." *Human Biology*, volume 5, no. 3, pp. 313-370.

[1] As National Research Fellow in the Biological Sciences, I am indebted to the National Research Council for the opportunity to undertake this work, and to my sponsors, Dr. E. A. Hooton of Harvard University and Dr. A. V. Kidder of the Carnegie Institution and the Laboratory of Anthropology at Santa Fe. I am also indebted to the Division of Anthropology of Harvard University, and especially to its chairman, Dr. A. M. Tozzer, for a grant of funds which enabled me to accompany the expedition in the field.
[2] S. D. — standard deviation.   C. V. — coefficient of variation.

[3] Undesignated as to sub-adult or adult classification.

Chapter Nine - Yaqui Agriculture

Richard Arthur Studhalter

History of Yaqui Agriculture

The terms *agriculture* and *war* come very close to being antonyms. A war-loving people has neither time nor opportunity to develop that backbone of civilization — agriculture. The war drums take all of the able bodied away from home and, when the battles rage near at hand, agricultural pursuits become both dangerous and impossible. War, the roving spirit, is antagonistic to agriculture, the sedentary spirit. We have heard the story of Civil War veterans who carried valuable seeds through the holocaust sewn into their clothing, in order that crops might be planted and agriculture be restored after the smoke had cleared away. War and agriculture are, indeed, antonyms.

In exactly the same spirit, the terms agriculture and Yaqui may be said to be antonyms. What more war-loving race has there been on the American continent than the Yaqui Indians? For a period of about four centuries they have been on an almost constant war path with the Spaniards and the Mexicans, and they are still spoken of as the only unconquered Indians in America. For about four hundred years they have been driven, more or less periodically, from their eight villages, abandoning homes and fields in pursuit either of the enemy or of safety in the adjacent Bacatete Mountains. What stories of devastation one could write, what stories of reconstruction, of hunger, of obtaining seeds for the next year's crops, seeds which must often have been worth almost their weight in gold — if one only knew such details of a forgotten history through four long centuries! The last Yaqui uprising occurred only six years ago, and one is not at all certain that there will be no more of them.

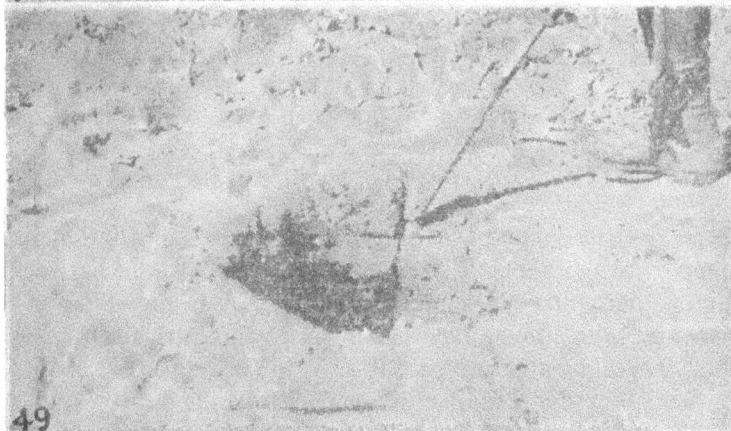

Plate 14
48. Yaqui agricultural implements.
49. A melon pit recently planted. Note the cross etched on the side of the hole;
this is to keep evil away.
50. A field of beans and corn.

Agriculture is, nevertheless, the very heart of the civilization of the Yaqui Indians. It is now in the ascendency, partly because a peace — or at least a truce — has been declared between the Yaquis and the Mexicans, and partly because four centuries of relentless selection have weeded out the most warlike blood and left a larger proportion of peace-tolerant, sedentary, agricultural strains among this remarkably independent race of Indians. This agriculture, as old as their race, will in the future have a better opportunity of growing into a healthy infant, of which its parents may yet be proud.

Not too much is known about the agricultural pursuits of the ancient Yaqui Indians. That they were agriculturists was stressed by Perez de Ribas, a missionary who worked among them in the first half of the seventeenth century. Important as were their agricultural pursuits, these can hardly be said to have constituted a rapidly developing program; or indeed not a conscious program at all. Modern Yaqui agriculture had its beginning only a few years ago when, with the signing of a treaty of peace, the Mexican government made an honest effort to help the Indians in becoming a peaceful, sedentary, agricultural tribe. They were encouraged to improve their crops, and farm implements of many kinds were made available to them. (Figure 48, Plate 14). This effort was successful to such an extent that the Indians purchased in 1926, an immense ditch digger or canal digger at the enormous cost of 15,000 pesos. Unfortunately, this fine piece of machinery was abandoned with the next uprising, before it was completely assembled, and is now rusting along the railroad track at Vicam Switch, Sonora. It represents an unfinished and decadent monument to a surprisingly progressive community spirit.

At the present time, then, Yaqui agriculture is a queer mixture of the old and new. One may expect many of the ancient methods to remain as part of the heritage of the race. On the other hand, the signs of Mexican help and influence can be easily read into the colorful practices of crop growing. This paper will deal with conditions as they are at present, and will make little effort to segregate the ancient from the modern. The conditions discussed are those found near the two villages of Vicam and Torin, in the State of Sonora.

The Agricultural Environment

The Yaqui farms lie on or near the Rio Yaqui, in a dry, subtropical climate, comparable in some measure to that of the lower Rio Grande. The rainfall, never abundant, comes mostly during the summer, with a secondary fall in the middle of the winter. The temperature varies rather considerably, as it does in most dry regions. It is excessively high in summer, but not damagingly low in winter. The number of days with sunshine must be very large indeed.

Yaqui agriculture is a sand agriculture. Little variation is found in this sea of sand, except that back from the river at a distance of a mile or more is found a somewhat greater admixture of clay which, during dry seasons, forms a very fine and penetrating powder.

But even in the driest season and in the driest soil, a moist subsoil in reached at a depth of six or eight inches. Along the river banks, the water table, of course, is a little lower.

Land Ownership and Clearing of Land

Virtually every adult Yaqui male is a farmer. (Figure 54, Plate 15). If a young man is not fortunate enough to inherit a farm, all he needs to do is select a piece of raw land, clear it, plant a crop — and by common consent the land is his just as long as he uses it.

Perhaps his biggest task is the clearing of the land. Depending on the location he has selected, he must get rid of cacti, mesquite trees, willows, cottonwoods, or the bamboo-like *carrizo*. The cacti range all the way from the small but vicious *cholla* to the large organ pipes and the giant *sahuaras*. The stems of all of these are cut into short lengths with an axe or machete and the roots are dug out; after drying in piles in the sun for several weeks, the plants are burned. The trees, whether willow, cottonwood, or mesquite, are handled much as would be done in this country, even to the ringing or girdling of the trunks. Getting rid of the rapidly growing *carrizo*, however, presents a different problem. It is easy enough to cut down the above-ground succulent stems with a sharp hoe or a double-edged weeder; but the large tough underground rhizome or rootstock must be grubbed out or plowed — a task which usually requires two or three years for a complete riddance.

The *carrizo* plant of the Yaquis is technically called *Arundo Donax*; the common name in the United States is giant reed. Although this tall grass is bamboo-like, it belongs to the tribe Festuceae rather than to the bamboo tribe, Bambuseae. It is a native of the Mediterranean region, where it is used for wickerwork and matting. In the United States it is often grown for ornament. In the South ,and especially in the more arid Southwest, it has escaped cultivation and become naturalized. In the Yaqui region it grows to be quite tall, often reaching a height of 25 to 30 feet, and it forms dense thickets along the water courses, particularly en sandy soil. (Figure 52, Plate 15).

The size of farms varies a good deal, depending mostly on the available land and the nearness of water. For the spring crop, a man usually plants from three to ten acres; in the summer and fall, when more wet ground is available, one man (which really means one family) may till from five to twenty acres. After all, more land would mean more work, and the Yaqui is afflicted with the native manana inertia of the Indian and Mexican peons.

The small size of the individual fields is even more surprising. A wheat field may range from one-fourth to two acres; a field of English peas from one-half to one acre; of *garbanzo* up to two or three acres; of corn up to three or four acres; and of watermelon from a single pit to one acre. Several kinds of crops may occupy a single row, or even a single pit, and on a single acre may be found a dozen different crops. One entire tobacco crop was found to consist of 32 plants, and a sugar-cane crop and a sweet potato crop of even fewer individuals. On one hillside farm some 40 feet wide and 150 feet long were found in the spring of 1934 fifteen distinct crops, as follows: corn, beans, watermelons, onions, garlic, *garbanzos,* tomatoes, *cilantro,* tobacco, sugar cane, *mango,* sweet potatoes, anise, mustard, and a garnish plant called *sacculanto.*

Most of the fields are fenced. The posts are made of any available timber, of which there are several kinds, and the wire is usually barbed. The number of wires in a fence varies from one to three. At times one man's farm is separated from that of another by an unplowed strip of land three or four feet wide.

Land inheritance is not a complicated problem. Yaqui law, all of which is of course unwritten, decrees that when a man dies, the land goes to his widow, provided he and his wife had had a church wedding. If the wife is dead, it goes to the oldest son. If there are no sons, it passes to the oldest daughter, provided she is married. If none of these conditions applies, it goes to other relatives.

The Water Problem

The greatest individual agricultural problem of the Yaquis is water. As long as the Rio Yaqui flowed in its natural course and carried all its water through its own channel to the Gulf of California, there was sufficient water for all agricultural pursuits. But with the diversion of all the water (except during the rainy season) into the Obregón canal to feed a newly developed agricultural area to the south of Yaquiland, the Yaqui Indians have been left during most of the year with only a few scattered water-holes in their wide river-bed. There is, then, at the present time a greater dependence on the meager rainfall than formerly. Fortunately the flatness and sandiness of the country insure that most of the rainfall sinks into the ground.

A number of crops are grown without irrigation. Among those are wheat, English peas and *garbanzos* as spring crops, and corn and watermelons as fail crops. The roots do not need to penetrate deeply into the soil to reach water.

Irrigation is carried on in two ways, by canals and by the carrying of water by man-power. Throughout the Yaqui region there are small irrigation-ditches running for several miles from the banks of the river. Since the diversion of the river water, however, these canals have remained dry except during the summer rains; even during the second half of September, 1934, when there was a considerable amount of water in the river, all canals seen were dry. The irrigation-ditches, therefore, are now of relatively little value to the Indians.

The carrying of water in buckets has only a limited use, but it is universally done in the spring of the year. The source of the water is the occasional water-hole in the river at this season, or wells dug in the sand. The latter are dug deeper as the dry season advances, and are usually rectangular in shape.

Either water is hoisted up by bucket on one end of a rope, or else a narrow stairstep is cut into the moist sand down to the water-level.

The water is carried in buckets, one bucket being hooked to either end of a short pole carried across the shoulder in the same fashion as appears to be done nearly the world over. For household purposes, however, the women, who do none of the field work except during harvest times, prefer to carry a bucket of water on their heads. In almost all cases, the buckets are the rectangular five-gallon tin cans used by the oil companies in the automobile trade; the can is made ready for use by cutting out the top and by nailing a rounded wooden handle into the upper part.

Water is often carried only a few feet, but the less fortunate farmer must go greater distances. In the drought of 1934 many # wells ran dry, and in some cases water was carried a mile or two in buckets for certain crops, especially watermelons.

Some General Agricultural Practices

Due in part to the water situation, the spring and the fall crops are handled somewhat differently. Some of the spring crops, such as wheat, English peas, *garbanzos,* and *cilantro,* are put into the ground in November or December and need only the very meager winter rains to bring them to maturity in May. Such crops are planted in plowed fields.

Other crops, such as corn and watermelon, are planted in the late winter in shallow pits (Figure 49, Plate 14) and are watered by hand until the plants are quite large. These crops also mature in May.

A third type of culture is used mainly for onions and garlic. A level sandy area ranging in size from two feet square to eight by twelve feet, is enclosed by a dirt wall, four to five inches high. Water is poured in from buckets. On occasion this plan is also used for other crops as tomatoes, tobacco, and sugar-cane.

A fourth group of crops is that planted after the summer rains, to mature in November. Corn is by all odds the outstanding member of this group, which is at that season almost invariably planted in plowed fields and either receives no water other than rain water, or else is given some supplementary water from the irrigation canals.

Plowing, which is never done deeply, is practiced twice a year, in January or February, and again in the summer. We were told that one man can plow one acre in two days. Horses are available for this work.

Cultivation is done to an extent, often only once for a crop.

Crop rotation is not practiced intentionally. Land is occasionally left fallow, but again not by design; it is known, however, that this helps to improve the land.

Plate 15
51. A homemade harrow.
52. A "carrizo" (a bamboo-like cane or giant reed) thicket along the Yaqui River.
53. A cross erected on the bank of the Yaqui River to prevent the water from cutting into a field.
54. A Yaqui farmer.

The Yaqui farmer saves his own seed. At the time of planting, the seed is never pre-soaked. Tomatoes and onions are the only crops transplanted, and this is by no means done universally.

All harvesting is done by hand, and often in a very primitive manner. Of especial interest are the harvesting and winnowing of wheat and of *garbanzos,* the method being quite similar to that used in biblical times.

Some of the harvest is stored by the farmer for his own use; but too often, it is said, he sells his harvest to the Mexican traders and buys it again in small quantities as he needs it, at a greatly augmented price.

Some Individual Crops

Yaqui agriculture is, almost of necessity, limited to the culture of annual plants. With an uprising always looming this side of the horizon, any agricultural pursuit is difficult enough; and it would surely take a brave and optimistic Yaqui to plant a fruit-tree, the initial crop of which is several years in the future. For this reason, perennials of all kinds are almost completely absent in Yaquiland. It is, however, an indication of progress that a few fruit-trees are gradually coming to the attention of several forward-looking Yaqui farmers, the chief of these being citrus fruits, mangos, pomegranates, and date-palms.

The absence of grapes might be explained on the same basis as that of other perennials; but no explanation can apparently be given for the complete absence of cotton, except the difficulty of ginning and marketing. This absence of cotton is all the more noticeable since, according to Perez de Ribas, cotton was grown by the Yaquis during the first half of the seventeenth century; from it they made cloth mantles.

The major crop is without question corn. Watermelons, wheat, *frijoles,* white beans, string beans, *garbanzos,* English peas, onions, and garlic are also of major importance.

Other crops are as follows: tomato, pumpkin, *cilantro,* tobacco, potato, sweet potato, chili peppers (which are not generally liked by the Yaquis), sugar-cane, anise, mango, and canteloupe. The total number of crops raised by the Yaquis is about thirty.

A few words should be said concerning some of the more important individual crops.

Corn (maize) is planted both as a spring and fall crop. (Figure 50, Plate 14). As a spring crop, it is planted in the winter months (there being apparently no definite time); and it matures, after a season of slow growth, in May or June. In the spring most of the plants are grown in pits dug by hand, rather than in furrows made by the plow. This is associated with the small winter rainfall and with the greater ease of watering a pit. Many of the fields are as close to the river as possible to facilitate the carrying of irrigation water. The pits are generally about four feet apart, each pit containing three to five plants. When it is planted in plowed fields the furrows are about four feet apart. At the end of March, plants said to be four months old were found to be about three feet tall, and not yet in tassel.

The fall crop of corn is planted in August, after the summer rains are about over. The fields of this, the most important of all the fall crops, are further from the river than is the case with many of the fields used in the spring, the benches near the river's edge being now too wet and too much in danger of being overflowed. Growth is more rapid at this season of the year and plants come to maturity in November. In the autumn, plowed fields are used exclusively, except when the scarcity of water makes the use of pits more profitable. On September 20, the corn plants were three to nine feet high and were in all stages from those just beginning to tassel out to those in which pollination had been completed.

Harvesting was not seen for any of the crops, since both our spring and fall visits were made too early in the season. Ears of corn were not seen hanging in the Yaqui homes, as is so often the case among other Indians of the Southwest. Shelled corn is stored in sacks or in mat bins; we were told of underground storage pits, used when the crop is unusually large, but none of these was seen. The seed for the next crop is usually stored in sacks.

Several varieties of beans are grown by the Yaquis, including *frijoles,* string beans, and limas. (Figure 50, Plate 14). The first type is the most common. All the varieties are grown either in plowed fields or in pits; the former may range up to two acres in extent. There is both a spring and a fall crop. Sometimes beans are threshed and winnowed in the same manner as will be presently described for the *garbanzo.* The seeds are stored in sacks or in mat bins, and occasionally in underground pits.

The Yaquis are apparently just as fond of watermelons as are other Indians in the Southwest. This plant is not extensively grown in the fall of the year, but constitutes one of the major crops noted in the spring. The seeds are planted almost exclusively in pits (at least such was the case during the very dry season of 1934), these being ten to fifteen feet apart. (Figure 49, Plate 14). Corn and watermelon are often planted together in the same pit. Planted in January and maturing in May, the vines are said to grow to a length of 12 or 15 feet. Five or six seeds are planted in each pit, which is at first vertically walled and with a flat bottom, like a broad U; as the vines grow in length, the pit is scraped down to the form of a shallow wide open V. Vines two months old were 10 to 30 inches in length, some of them with three of four open flowers. No fruit was seen, but we were told of at least two varieties, a spherical and an oblong type. Seeds for the next crop are often stored in *tequila* bottles.

The planting of wheat is done by hand, immediately behind the plow, in November and December. The only moisture received comes from the meager winter rains. The soil at the river's edge is not suitable for wheat, the fields of which are found from one to three miles from the river, chiefly at Vicam village. Harvesting is done by hand with a sickle or a small scythe.

Threshing is done on a dirt floor some twenty feet in diameter, which has been wetted and made smooth and hard. Horses, which are owned by "all the wheat farmers," are driven over the wheat tops on the floor until the threshing is complete. If horses are not available, the tops are beaten with mesquite or other poles, after which they are removed by hand and the winnowing done during a wind with a large wooden shovel. The method is very much like those portrayed in pictures of biblical times.

Garbanzo beans or chick pea (*Cicer arietium*), introduced from the Old World, has become rather an important crop at Vicam village. Its importance was no doubt enhanced by the active interest of ex-president Obregón, who is said to have made himself the *garbanzo* king of Mexico, growing a large part of the entire Mexican crop on his estate just south of the Yaqui River and controlling the distribution of the remainder. The Yaquis call the plant "Spanish bean." It is planted in November and ripens in May. Grown in the same soil as wheat, the plants not only furnish in their seeds some of the protein eaten by the Yaquis, but in. addition their tender tips are broken off, boiled, and eaten as greens. They are grown in plowed fields of fair extent (one-half to three acres). Their harvesting, as described to us, is of particular interest, reminding one of the post-cultural care of wheat. The entire plants are pulled up and permitted to dry from one-half to one day on a hard smooth dirt floor, such as is used for the threshing of wheat. The dried plants are now raked away and the pods winnowed from the seeds during a wind by a very large wooden shovel. Seeds are stored in sugar or flour sacks to be eaten at any time during the year.

English peas are grown in very much the same manner as are the *garbanzos*.

It is quite strange that the Yaqui does not share the love for cultivated flowers which is so pronounced in the Mexican peon. The familiar tin cans of geraniums in the window sills of the peon are virtually absent in Yaquiland. Only in two instances were cultivated plants noted in a Yaqui home.

Agricultural Implements

The agricultural implements of the Yaquis are both primitive and advanced, both home-made and factory-made (Figure 48, Plate 14). Many of the latter are of Mexican manufacture, and perhaps even more of them came from the United States.

Home-made wooden plows are said to be still in use, although we saw none of them. Except for the double-edged weeders and the various kinds of handles, the number of home-made implements is small. One fairly pretentious steel-pronged home-made harrow was seen near Vicam (Figure 51, Plate 15).

The bulk of the agricultural tools and implements probably date mostly from the period of the last peace treaty, at which time the Mexican government began seriously to encourage Yaqui agriculture and to make many implements available to the Indians. All of the implements are of simple design. They were mostly made in the United States, and many a familiar trade-mark can be found on shovels, rakes, machetes, axes and plows. Some of these were probably brought into Yaquiland by families returning from a sojourn in the United States. At least one mystery has received no solution: namely, the presence of a United States Army wagon, in good condition and with the United States stamp untouched, in front of a Yaqui home in Torin.

Insects, Plant Diseases, Plant Pest

The Yaqui makes little or no distinction between insect pests and plant disease; to him these are all "bugs". In most instances the Indian takes his loss stoically, and no effort is made to improve a situation which seems hopeless. Thus, rabbits are at times a serious pest, but nothing is done to keep them away except the occasional practice of keeping children (both boys and girls) posted in the fields during the day to drive away the rabbits and birds with bows and arrows or with sling-shots.

Javelinas are killed with a bow and arrow, or else rounded up with the aid of dogs and killed with stones thrown by hand. Some small animals are trapped, some of the traps being of unique native design.

Scarecrows are fairly common. A waving rag is tied to the top of a *carrizo* pole and the latter stuck in the field. Or a similar pole may have an old straw hat on it. Or two or three poles may be used together, one with a rag and another with a hat. The writer's own impression is that these devices are just as efficient as our own more elaborate scarecrows — and just as inefficient.

There seems to be no knowledge at all of insecticides and fungicides, and the idea that some birds might help a crop by eating injurious insects is apparently unknown.

Some Agricultural Superstitions

Insects and plant diseases are not, however, given a free hand without a combat by the only methods known to the Yaquis — practices which we must rank as agricultural superstitions.

When a few watermelon or pumpkin or corn seeds are dropped into a pit, and some loose sand scraped over the unsoaked seed, some wood ashes are sprinkled around the seed in the form of a circle some four or five inches in diameter. That this will ward off some insects can be readily believed; but it is difficult to follow the supposed effectiveness for many weeks, since the wind soon covers the wood ashes with sand and the two or three bucketfuls of water poured into the pit every few days spread the ashes over a larger area.

Again, old corn stalks, particularly partially burned stalks, are believed to have mysterious power. Two or three of them stuck into a pit or merely laid across the top of it, are believed to keep away the *javelinas* and other ani-

111

mals. A *carrizo* stalk is also effective. The stalk must be dead; green ones are not satisfactory. Perhaps the burning of the stalk is a foreboding of disaster to the j*avelina*.

Miraculous powers are assigned to the cross— a remnant of mediaeval superstition still found the world over. After planting in a pit, the sign of the cross is scratched with a finger into the sand in the bottom, or into the sandy perpendicular side wall. (Figure 49, Plate 14). This will keep away insects and diseases and any other evil.

Last September we came suddenly upon a cross made of weeds tied together and fastened to the wires of a fence. (Figure 53, Plate 15). The cross was about two feet long and a foot wide, and was fastened so as to face the steep river bank only a few feet away. The river was rapidly undermining the bank and approaching the field. The owner believed that his field would be perfectly safe from undermining, for what mere body of raging water could pass the sign of the cross?

But let us be kind to the Yaqui; he is doing the best he can. While to us some of his practices are quite amusing, we should be careful with the throwing of stones lest we be reminded of the glass houses in which our ancestors, not very far distant, lived, and of the all-too-common practice of the white man of today of letting that wise old man in the moon determine the time of planting. After all, the Yaqui Indian has derived some of his superstitions from the white man. How many of our own present cherished practices will be laughed at in a century or two?

Appendix A - The Life and Doings of the Yaqui Indians of the San Ygnacio Yaqui River

as furnished to Ivan Williams, of the U. S. Border Patrol, Immigration Service, Tucson, Arizona, by General Guadalupe Flores, of Pascua Village, Tucson, Arizona, written by Juan Amarillas, Yaqui historian.

(Editor's note: The following account is printed as given by Juan Amarillas. It is inconsistent in places and at times does not make sense, but we find it difficult to edit the paper without changing its content. The original version, written in Yaqui, was translated into Spanish by Juan Amarillas. The Spanish version was then translated into English by Ivan Williams.)

In the year 1523 [?] went those who were met in the north for the motive of baptism, because during this time there was no baptism known here and for this reason people did not want to be baptized as this was the custom of their forefathers.

The racial characteristics at that time were as follows: Study of ancient apparel, Dances, Punches (a drink), Jigs, and a dance called "The deer and the Coyote". The Yaqui Indians revolt of 1740 began the writing of this history by Juan Vanderas, a fierce writer. Before this, historians were destroyed at the beginning of the revolt.

From the accommodations of these fierce pages comes the history of the Yaqui Indians of Sonora, Mexico, histories that for their interest and attractions deserve to be reported in this special edition, which contain many more diversified businesses; related as a unit importance in general on this race, discovering them to be of a natural quick talent, that is, with but very little coaching. When once learned, all kinds of mechanical occupations are retained. Among these occupations we find plasterers, blacksmiths, carpenters, coppersmiths, fire work workers and all other occupations known in the country. There are equally as many players of the violin and harp, learned through their own talent without even the first rule of note or music.

They are of a firm character, and no one can separate them when they plan to keep a secret or realize a project. No people could equal the Yaquis during this century of mystery, secret and enterprise. These people would rather be killed than reveal what they believe a secret and their own affair, and this characteristic is the determining force of their ability to keep resolutions, when they believe that they have been deceived, and when once deceived, they treat all deceivers a certain way.

In general the Yaquis are distinct of other races, yet in some cases there are some exceptions for some are reared among the whites and cultivated to the whites way of thinking, even so, they are in sympathy with the Yaquis customs.

We of the Yaqui tribe, so say our people of ancient times, are the direct descendants of two of the oldest known inhabitants of the great land, our historians who did not start making history until the 12th century know very little of the inhabitants before then, but we have been told that from the beginning of time that the two great tribes roamed through the valleys and the mountains, the one great tribe was of little people and the other great tribe was of giants. The little people lived in the mountains and the big people lived in the valleys. At one time a great calamity struck the little people in the mountains and they fled to the valleys and mingled with the giants and from this sprang the Yaqui tribe.

The Yaquis are of a bronze color, are well built in stature and can stand great endurance. I he women are fleshy and of medium stature, there are some women in the villages that are white in color and are very beautiful, they are the daughters of the so called "Coyotes" they are the offsprings of a Spanish father and an Indian mother, their language is quite different, very clear, easy to learn and susceptible to grammatical rules.

But now we enter the picturesque part of this history. In the year 1740, all the towns of the Yaqui river revolted, because of what the criminals who had fled from prison told them when they came there. These men introduced among them inspired ideas to overthrow the government, making them believe that the government was attempting to take away their land. They united into large masses, 700 into one group, 800 into another and 1000 into another, all armed to fight the government, D. Agustin Vindascola who represented them. In one group of 700 men in the first battle on the Tambos Mountains a distance of half way between Tacaipia and Suague. They went into action with beating drums, blowing horns and with much festivity attending the multitude.

There was a Spanish leader at the head of the government troops against the Yaquis, but the Yaquis fought with much courage, and killed over 2000 men putting them to flight, after a few days of fighting. Several days elapsed before they met again, this time in the Atoncahue Mountains. This time the government were in greater number of men and better prepared, they suffered their defeat, leaving over 2000 dead on the battle field which was a horrible example. The balance of them surrendered themselves and asked for peace, they conceded and following this Vindascola made them give him the leader of the revolt who was executed. This encounter resulted in peace for the Tribe which lasted for eighty-five years, from 1740-1825, after which time they again arose in rebellion committing frightful assassinations in towns and ranches. From the year 1825 one can say that the Yaquis were in constant rebellion, although they have enjoyed a few intervals of peace during this period, being at all times conspicuous and always independent of all governments.

In 1826 they repeated their revolt, this and the one of the past year was caused by a cunning Indian by name of Juan Vanderas, who with false super-

stitions deceived the people, making them believe that the Virgin of Guadalupe talked with him and that She was inspiring all his preachings to them. In
the year 1832 there arose new revolts by the same leader Vanderas, who
received lame and vote from the public. He talked favorably with over a
thousand whites who he guided to the towns of Opotas and Pimas via Soyopa
with the idea of gathering all the Opoterias. In this state he left the city of
Hermosillo with a crowd of neighbors which consisted of 100 cavalrymen on
orders of D. Leonardo Escalante who at this date was officially retired, and
on the way he united with another troop of neighbors from the town of
Matape, Tecoripa and other points, organizing a division of three or four
hundred men with which he marched to overtake the rebels. In the same
town, Soyopa, he saw them at the time that Chief Vanderas was encamped on
the other side of the river at the water spring of San Antonio de la Huerta.
They engaged in a battle with the Indians who, after resisting them for three
hours were defeated leaving the camp full of corpse and among the corpse
was the body of D. N. Cacillas, neighbor of Tepic, of a good family who, like
the leader, was with the Yaquis. At the same time that this happened Vanderas was taken prisoner by his neighbor D. Ignacio Calmeneraro and others
in San Antonio and together with native Opota who was second to Vanderas
in this revolt. They were conducted to the Capitol of Arizpe where they were
executed. Previous to the execution the first one to speak declared that their
plans were to exterminate the Department, thus the revolution started and
they destroyed the Department. There were many horrible assassinations of
women and children and according to the accounts of the historians some of
the innocent were held by the feet and their heads hit upon rocks, thus killing them, this happened at the ranch Despensa, where they finished with the
family of Encinas consisting of 11 persons including two babies. Some prisoners were put on a mark and shot, others were hung from trees and shot,
others were stood off a distance and shot with bows and arrows, filling their
bodies with a multitude of arrows until they dropped, leaving the unfortu-
nates making frightful moments of desperations. All these orders were carried out in this frightful revolt which makes a very bad history in the exam-
ples of the savages which in no doubt was carried to all the world. In the year
1842 during the month of June, the day before the Estallar, the first revolution called the Gandaras, they killed with sticks and arrows in the town of
Cocori, the mayor of this own race with only the motive of jealousy in com-
pliment his duty. He excused the robbers, among these robbers were stolen a
certain number of cows, who were stolen from a neighbor, who reclaimed
them, this mayor made them return them. A few days after this they united a
band of armed men (thieves) 44 in number and suddenly entered at 7 o'clock
in the morning, Coccri, with the intentions of killing the mayor, while a number of the neighbors looked on who were there at this time. The same thing
happened to General Juan Maria Juracamea, whose history is well known of

Indian influence and wicked support the cause of the government with no other reason but to correct the robberies was assassinated in the year 1843.

Notwithstanding the bad qualities it is necessary them due justice, which are the only people of Mexico for the working of the mines and the fields or the camps construction of edificies and the rest of the occupation of one society all these employees are manifested in a simple and rare way of doing it. They do what they are told to do firmly, their enterprise and are audacity in war.

We do not know the exact year but believe it was the year 1863 when Frances fought in Hermosillo with the Federals of Mexico, there Refugio Tanori defended him with the Yaqui workers, with Pimas and all the smaller tribes, they defeated the Federals of the Government and then desired to go to the Yaqui River. They reached Pitaya [Pitahaya] one mile from the town of Belen and here he left everything that belonged to Frances. They left his armies, ammunitions and powder for their defence. This is where the Mexicans began to hate the Yaquis because they defended Frances. In 1875 a company of Yaquis was organized by Frances. In this year the people of the government of Mexico came here and here in Pitaya fought the Yaquis with the Federals. Pepe Pesquerira and Pepe Mariscal retreated because he was running out of men and upon reaching Guaymas he sent a peace message to the Yaquis but with always the idea of killing the Yaquis. In 1877 he fought with the Yaquis again, the Yaquis won this time also and again he sent a peace message. After this there was a new General named Jose Marie Cajeme of the Yaqui Tribe of the eight towns. After this the eight towns had many animals, cattle, horses and all kinds of animals of which there were more than a million head. These were all taken away from the Yaquis by the Federal government and this is why we are so poor. This statement we know. And in the year 1885 he returned again and Frances arrived and fought with the Yaquis on the out skirts of the town of Uican (what they call anllil) here they defeated him again and killed many people, they fled again to Guaymas and again they sent a written note asking for peace, but peace was not accepted this time. In the year 1887 the government troops returned again to fight the Yaquis, this time Topete, Lorenzo Torres and Luis Torres were here. General Luis Torres committed a great treason among the Yaquis tribes, the Indian Cajeme took all the people of the eight towns to the mountains, here he committed a great treason, he had women and children among the men. Here the govt, troops partly defeated the Yaquis. Here many people of the Yaqui tribes were destroyed and killed, they killed many families and little children, boys and innocent people. Here they [?] Indian Cajeme with all the honors of the Yaquis. He took all the flags and Testano and everything else they had. He left here climbing the mountains and went direct to Alemito. Here they slept and the next morning they went straight to Bacateiito and at noon rested there, they had with them two escorts and that evening they went to Guicori and from there went out of the boundary line and reached

116

Tinaja de Tierra and here slept in a plain called "Mateo", and here he hid the honors of the tribe and at midnight he made belief that he had to... [attend to the necessities of nature]. He left and did not return. In the morning the escorts picked up his trail and followed him to the mountains of Boco Bierto [Boca Abierta]. He passed straight through Chillitepin and went straight to Cocori by the sea. He passed by Batamotal and here crossed the railroad tracks and entered an old adobe house, to this point the escorts followed him. He left here for the ranch of Guaymas and then he reached the house of a washer-woman, and this washerwoman was the one who discovered him and his whereabouts. Here they caught him and took him to Guaymas, together with the honors of the Yaqui tribe, and at the same time Juan Tetabiate was made General of the Yaqui tribe, and in the year 1898 they made peace in the station of Ortiz. Then Senior Francisco Peinao gave Juan Tetabiate and the eight towns peace. And in the year 1900 he attacked Juan Tetabiate at Masocoba and made him his comrade in battle against his will. There was a multitude of people, they fought like drunk people, stabbing each other. Here many Yaquis were killed. The people of the Government killed many of the Yaqui tribe, they killed women, and children and babies, all these died in this fight. Here started the most terrific battle among those in the mountains they were unable to do any thing to these people. Then again in 1904 they started fighting with the Yaqui workers, he began to take the workers and ship them away, others were hanged underneath their houses. He also shipped many to other distant points.

In the year 1909 the Generals Rafael Isabel, Lorenzo and Luis Torres and General Barron gave peace to the Yaquis through General Luis Buli. They brought him and his Yaqui men from the mountains, but still Senior Juan Jose Sibaluame never did come down from the mountains to this date so says Jesus Roja of Sibaluame. In the Year 1910 the revolts started again by reason of Francisco Madero. They completely defeated the Yaquis who were in the mountains.

In the Year 1920 Senior Adolfo de la Huerta made peace with the Yaqui Ignacio Mori and with the General Matos and also with the General Luis Espinosa, these were the Yaquis who led their native tribes. In 1926, the 12th day of September, they got him as a prisoner of war. Luis Matos took General Obregon in the canyons with the pretense of not wanting to be seen by any people of the eight towns, he made General Obregon believe that he was a traitor to his tribe, he told him that he would lead his men to where all of them could be captured, after they got to the deep canyon, Luis Matos took General Obregon to another place to tell him some secrets and there he was captured as a prisoner of war, they held him for 24 hours and on the night of the 13th day General Manzo came to defend him. The TRAITOR Matos went to the mountains and stayed there until he was freed by the people in the mountains, after much fighting with General Manzo. General Manzo had 1000 men and they fought at the station of Ortaz. There they killed many of

General Manzos men and in December they began fighting with airplanes, with the Yaquis that were in the mountains and three airplanes were burned one fell at Guas Nueva, three miles from Bacatete. On the 1st day of January ObregOn came again with the Cavalry and made an agreement with the people of the mountains to stop the fighting of the people of the mountains and General Manzo, but Luis Matos did nothing but take their families and in 1927 they started to come north. In April they started and reached Mesquital at day break. The 32 men began fighting against the 1115 men at Planceas with the General Alselmo Armenta, and after some more were coming, but these were turned back, although a few remained.

Because of all these experiences we have suffered a lot, this Senor Williams, is all the history that we have at hand so says Juan Amarillas, who wrote this history.

Appendix B

A written statement given by a delegation of Yaqui chiefs to members of the expedition at Torin in April, 1934. The document, written in Spanish, was translated by Dr. C. B. Qualia.

In the years 1882, Porfirio Diaz, president of the Republic at that time declared baldia [national domain?] the territory of the Yaqui tribe, in order that many greedy persons might take possession of them, and the government aids them — with government troops to consummate the pillage. But the fact is that those Yaquis who rose up were never caught and the troops took vengeance on the peaceful [tame] ones, and on defenseless children and women, causing thus the peaceful Yaquis to rise in rebellion and then the troops perpetrated one of their worst deeds, of which even the American press gave an account, namely, they hanged many Yaqui women who were nursing children and when these women were in the throes of death, the milk issued from their bosoms. The military chieftains are indignant because they are constantly being taken by surprise and they take vengeance on the tame Yaquis who dedicate themselves to agriculture and who have no weapons with which to defend themselves. By night they attack their hamlets, killing women and children with their swords. [1] The Yaquis have possessed in common these lands, which amount to thirty thousand acres, from time immemorial. We raise on them abundant crops which permit us to live in absolute independence and with no need to do harm to anyone. These lands have tempted the covetousness of several speculators with the result that we have seen.

The governor at this time: Refugio Velceco.

The generals of Sonora: Martinez, Garcia, Lorenzo Torres, Louis Torres, Louis Medinas Harron, Topete Brabo Blanguet.

All the blood that has been shed served the cause of Louis Torres, Ramon Coral, Rafael Isobel, who are the caciques [political bosses] of Sonora and who in reality have directed the campaign against the Yaqui tribe.

May our American neighbors help us make known this trouble which has come to us.

In the year of 1926.

The idea of the Mexican Government. Calles and Obregon and A. Manso, against the Yaqui tribe in Sonora.

General Plutarco Elias Calles said: "It will be necessary to reelect me as many times as necessary, and I shall be re-elected. "The acknowledgement of the English debt has caused this...

"About to obtain a loan in Berlin, but in order to obtain it, I must continue in power, and I *shall* continue in power, but in order to establish Mexico's credit solidly, I must make peace — cost what it may. In future I shall brook no opposition in the chambers or in the governments of the states or in the *Camps* [military camps? or perhaps he means in rural districts?] Every one who rises up will be squelched without mercy. I must be absolute dictator, for I can allow no one to overshadow me, no one must overcome me. I must pass over the promises of Tustepec now, but later history will justify me, when men will all say that I gave lasting peace to Mexico, obtained credit, made foreign capital flow into this country, and when men see that I have carried to completion many public works and that in the coffers of the nation, millions are being accumulated and that all servants of the nation are paid and that the interest on the public debt is paid, then posterity will call me the hero of peace. All of this has not been good for Mexico."

We Indians say: The idea of our neighbors, the Mexicans, is merely to ruin our lands by cutting down timber without the permission of the Yaqui tribe; their idea is not to respect our rights, for if they did, there would be peace among the people.

[1] It is to be remembered that the Yaquis did not stand in need of lessons in cruelty. Perhaps, the Mexicans were trying to pay them back at this time in their own medicine. However that may be, the memories of the Yaquis are long. They have avenged themselves of this and other acts of cruelty on the part of the Mexicans with compound interest. As late as 1930 a group of mountain Yaquis raided the ranches to the northeast of the Bacatete Mountains in the vicinity of the Slaughter ranch. On a Mexican ranch adjoining the Slaughter ranch, they killed a Mexican girl about sixteen. They drove a crowbar through her neck and swung her in a well. Before they left they gave her body a push so it would swing back and forth like a pendulum. When R. L. Slaughter, Jr. came by the place a short time later, she was still swinging. A few miles away the same party came upon a small Mexican boy about seven herding sheep. The Yaquis had with them about a dozen and a half case knives, such as are used for eating purposes on ranches. These they had got from a place they had recently ravaged. They pinned the boy's body to the ground by driving these knives through it. The boy's corpse was located days later by the buzzard's circling above it. On another excursion

the mountain Yaquis raided the Slaughter ranch one day while Mr. Slaughter and his cowboys were away on a round-up. The Indians plundered the house and took Mrs. Slaughter and a Mexican maid as prisoners. Mr. Slaughter later ransomed his wife and her maid for thirty saddle horses and twenty-four suits of blue denim overalls and jumpers.

Scores of similar instances, some of them quite recent, can be found in Sonora.

www.ingramcontent.com/pod-product-compliance
Lightning Source LLC
Chambersburg PA
CBHW022118280326
41933CB00007B/440